THE BIG BOOK OF FOOTBALL

BY MUNDIAL

ILLUSTRATED BY
DAMIEN WEIGHILL

WIDE EYED EDITIONS

CONTENTS

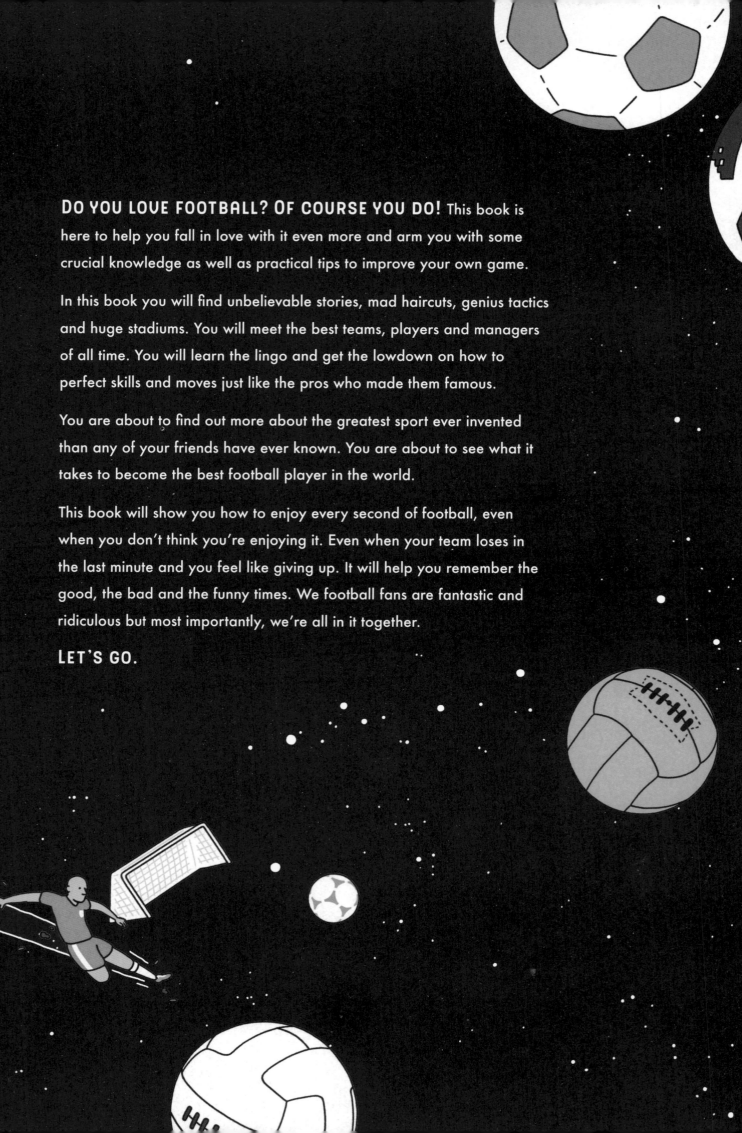

DO YOU LOVE FOOTBALL? OF COURSE YOU DO! This book is here to help you fall in love with it even more and arm you with some crucial knowledge as well as practical tips to improve your own game.

In this book you will find unbelievable stories, mad haircuts, genius tactics and huge stadiums. You will meet the best teams, players and managers of all time. You will learn the lingo and get the lowdown on how to perfect skills and moves just like the pros who made them famous.

You are about to find out more about the greatest sport ever invented than any of your friends have ever known. You are about to see what it takes to become the best football player in the world.

This book will show you how to enjoy every second of football, even when you don't think you're enjoying it. Even when your team loses in the last minute and you feel like giving up. It will help you remember the good, the bad and the funny times. We football fans are fantastic and ridiculous but most importantly, we're all in it together.

LET'S GO.

THE BASICS AND THE LINGO

Football is the best sport in the world because it's the simplest. From Brazil to Belgium, Bangladesh to Botswana, football is being played in every corner of the planet. Whether it's on a pitch, the street outside your house or the field down the road, you can play it anywhere.

All you need is a ball, or something that looks a bit like a ball. You can score great goals, make amazing passes and even win the World Cup (in your head) with a tennis ball, a load of scrunched up sticky tape or a pair of socks. Anybody, anywhere, anytime can play it.

BASIC LINGO

Here are the key phrases that will get you talking like a football expert in no time.

ASSIST
A pass, header or cross that comes just before a goal is scored. The German player Mesut Özil is the king of this.

BACKHEEL
A pass played with the back of a player's foot.

BICYCLE-KICK
With the ball behind them, a player throws their body into the air, makes a movement with the legs to get one in front of the other and connects with the ball to hit it over their head while in mid-air. Also known as an overhead kick.

BRACE
Two goals scored by the same player in one game.

CAPTAIN
The captain of the team is the leader on the pitch. They are chosen by the manager. You can recognise the captain by the armband they wear.

CHIP
Chipping the goalkeeper is when an attacker kicks the ball over the top of a goalkeeper's head and into the goal. When it works, it makes the person shooting look fantastic.

CLEAN SHEET
If a goalkeeper does not concede a goal (let a goal into the net), they have kept a 'clean sheet'. Before computers, scores would be recorded on a sheet of paper. And so, if the opposition didn't score, the sheet would be clean.

CORNER KICK

If a player kicks the ball out of play behind their own goal line, the opposition team get to kick the ball back into play from the corner of the pitch.

FOUL

When a player breaks the rules of the game. Punishable by a free kick or penalty.

CROSS

A delivery of the ball into the penalty area by the attacking team. Usually in the air, sometimes along the ground. England player David Beckham was the best at these.

FRIENDLY

A non-competitive game played between two teams just for fun or practice.

DRIBBLE

To run quickly with the ball at your feet.

HAT-TRICK

If one player scores three goals in the same game.

EXTRA TIME!

1-1

EXTRA TIME

If the scores in a football match are even at full time, it is called a **draw**. Sometimes, if a match ends in a draw, the teams will play for an extra 30 minutes (on top of the 90 they've already played) to try and determine a winner.

KICK-OFF

The very first kick of the game after the starting whistle blows.

FORMATION

This is the name given to the shape that a team takes during the match. For example, if a team plays four defenders, three central midfielders, two attacking midfielders and one striker, it looks a bit like a Christmas tree, so it is called 'The Christmas Tree Formation'. 4-4-2 is the standard formation.

NUTMEG

When another player rolls the ball through your legs. Humiliating, but brilliant.

OFFSIDE

Being caught 'offside' will result in the opposition being awarded a free kick. But what is it?

When your teammate passes the ball forward to you, there must be at least two opposition players between you and your opponent's goal at the moment your teammate passes. This is usually a defender and the goalkeeper. If there is only the goalkeeper between you and the goal at the moment the ball is passed to you, you are offside. If there is a defender and the goalkeeper between you and the goal when the ball is passed to you, you are onside.

ONSIDE | **OFFSIDE**

OWN GOAL

If you put the ball into the goal your team is defending, you have scored an 'own goal'. This counts as a goal for the opposition. Never mind, we've all done it.

POSSESSION

When a team is in control of the ball.

SAVE

A 'save' is when a goalkeeper prevents the opposition from scoring by stopping a shot from going into their team's goal. They have 'saved' their team. Thanks, goalie.

SHOOT

To 'shoot' means to kick the ball at the opposition goal. You take a 'shot' at the goal.

RED/ YELLOW CARD

A yellow card is a warning if you have committed a foul. If the referee shows you a red card, you have to leave the pitch, and you won't be allowed to play for the rest of the game. Two yellow cards have the same effect as a red card.

TACKLE

When you try to get the ball off another player.

STOPPAGE/ INJURY TIME

A normal football match lasts for 90 minutes. 'Stoppage' or 'injury' time is added to the end of a match to make up for the time when the game may have been stopped for any reason.

REFEREE

The person who is in charge of a match. They decide what counts as a foul or a goal, and they award red and yellow cards. If they blow their whistle, you have to stop playing and listen to what they say.

VOLLEY

When the ball is kicked before it has had a chance to bounce. Volleys look spectacular and are difficult to do.

STRANGER THINGS

In football, the basic terms are quite straightforward, but there are some very strange phrases. Here are a few of our favourites to add to your vocab.

JOURNEYMAN

A player who often changes club, never stopping at one for very long, as though they are on one long journey.

12TH MAN

You're only allowed 11 players on the pitch at one time, but if the crowd is being particularly loud and supportive, they can be described as the 12th man.

LOST THE DRESSING ROOM

Managers give pep talks in the dressing room. So if the players in a team no longer respect the manager, they have 'lost the dressing room'.

FERGIE TIME

Sir Alex Ferguson (Fergie) was the manager of the world-famous UK club Manchester United for a long time and tended to get what he wanted, including more stoppage time than usual. If a referee gives lots of stoppage time, it is called Fergie time.

MAGIC SPONGE

A quite ordinary sponge used by physios to treat injuries on the pitch. No one knows why or how it works, but we suspect it is magic.

FOX IN THE BOX

A player who is particularly effective in the penalty area. Dutch player Ruud van Nistelrooy was the foxiest in the box.

ONION BAG

Sometimes used to mean the goal because the netting looks a bit like a bag that onions come in.

GIANT-KILLING

When a small, low-ranked team unexpectedly beats a strong, famous team.

PARK THE BUS

When all the players in a team play in defensive positions. It is as though they have parked a double-decker in front of the goalposts.

HOSPITAL PASS

A pass from your own player that puts you in danger of losing the ball.

HISTORY OF FOOTBALL

Football is a game that has changed a lot over time in all sorts of ways. We're going to go on a whistle-stop tour through the big moments in football history and find out how we got from playing with a ball made of feathers to using high-tech footballs. Find out when the rules and techniques we use now were invented, from the introduction of new formations to playing 'Total Football'. See how particular players, managers and clubs changed the way the game was played, from Cruyff to Herrera, Messi to Puskás, Sir Bobby Robson to Olympique Lyonnais Féminin.

Let's see the big moments that have changed the game.

PUSKÁS

W

Football hasn't always been on TV and watched by millions of people. But, people have played football, or something very similar, for thousands of years. Here's how it all began and how over time it has changed and evolved into what we watch and play today.

Early beginnings It all started in China, over 2,000 years ago with a game called 'Ts'u-chü'. The ball was made of leather, and it was stuffed with animal hair and feathers. The goal was as tall as five grown-ups stood on each other's heads and as narrow as a child. As you can imagine, with a goal this shape, it was incredibly difficult to score and it was a very skilful game.

1925 The offside rule is changed so that only two opponents have to be between the attacker receiving the ball and the goal.

1920 On Boxing Day, Dick, Kerr Ladies beat St Helen's Ladies 4-0 in a game watched by 53,000 inside the stadium, with many more outside the stadium trying to get in. The FA became jealous of the huge crowds that women's matches were attracting, and in 1921, women's teams were banned from playing at men's club grounds. Thankfully, this ruling was overturned, but not until 1971. Now, whether you're a girl or boy you can become a world-class football superstar. Football is for everyone.

1929 Serie A is formed in Italy.

1928 La Liga is formed in Spain with the first season starting a year later.

1930 The first FIFA World Cup took place in Uruguay. The home team beat Argentina 4-2 in the final to become the first ever world champions.

1920 Egypt become the first African team to play in a competitive international match, losing 2-1 to Italy at the Olympics in Belgium.

1951 The first white football is used in an official game, instead of a traditional brown ball.

1956 Real Madrid win the first ever European Cup. They would go on to win many more.

1958 Edson Arantes do Nascimento, aka Pelé, wins his first World Cup with Brazil along with teammate Mané Garrincha. Brazil never lost a game in which Pelé and Garrincha played together.

1969 The Women's FA was formed following an increase in the popularity of football after the 1966 World Cup.

2019 FIFA estimated one billion people tuned in globally to watch the Women's World Cup, breaking the record by a huge margin and signalling that the sport is getting the long awaited attention it deserves.

2012 Lionel Messi scored 91 goals in a calendar year. That is, frankly, absurd. He might be an alien.

2010 The first World Cup to be hosted by an African nation was held in South Africa. Vuvuzelas (a type of horn) were blown by crowds and became iconic in the tournament.

2007 French team Olympique Lyonnais Féminin win the first of 13 consecutive league titles. They become the most dominant team in sporting history.

1500s In Europe, the earliest examples of a game similar to football began in the 1500s in a city called Florence, which is now in Italy. The game was called 'calcio' (pronounced 'caltch-yo'). There was no limit on how many people could play at once. Instead of a pitch, players chased a ball all over town. It was so violent, and so many people got hurt in the chaos, that it was eventually banned.

1700s A similar game called 'folk football' was played on the streets of London in the 1700s, but was also banned because of the serious injuries and damage it caused.

1862 The first professional football club, Notts County, was formed, and in the following year, the Football Association (the FA) was born. This is when the game started to shape properly.

1902 The penalty spot is invented. Before this, penalties were taken from anywhere along a line drawn 12 yards from the goal line.

1888
In 1888, the Football League was founded. The teams included Accrington, Aston Villa, Blackburn Rovers, Bolton Wanderers, Burnley, Derby County, Everton, Notts County, Preston North End, Stoke, West Bromwich Albion and Wolverhampton Wanderers. The first league title was won by Preston, who went the whole season without losing a game.

1912 Goalkeepers can no longer handle the ball outside of the penalty area.

1900s

1971 The FA lift the ban on women playing at 'men's' stadiums. The first ever women's FA Cup was held.

1991 China host the first Women's World Cup, with the USA overcoming Norway 2-1 in the final.

1992 The back pass rule is brought in. Goalkeepers are no longer allowed to pick up the ball with their hands if the ball is passed back to them by one of their own team, unless the ball is headed or chested to the goalie.

1970 Yellow and red cards are introduced.

2005 Liverpool were 3-0 down to A.C. Milan in the UEFA Champions League final in Istanbul. They pulled themselves together at half time and came back to draw 3-3. Liverpool then won 3-2 on penalties. The match is known as The Miracle of Istanbul.

2002 Brazil won their fifth World Cup, making them the nation with the most world cup wins.

2000 FIFA name Michelle Akers the Women's Player of the Century after winning two World Cups and one Olympic gold medal and pioneering the women's game.

1992 The Premier League is formed in England. The money in the game becomes huge.

1994 At the age of 42, Roger Milla becomes the oldest player ever to score at a World Cup at USA '94, and does a wiggly little dance at the corner flag to celebrate.

2000s

THE GREATEST TEAMS OF ALL TIME

Which is the greatest team of all time? This question causes arguments in playgrounds, at work and at the dinner table in every country, every day. It's impossible to find a perfect answer. This list is not definitive, and you may find teams you prefer for various reasons, but without doubt, these teams all made history in their own amazing way.

PRESTON NORTH END, UK
1888–89

This Preston North End team were invincible. They went a whole season without losing a single match. They did this 100 years before Arsène Wenger's Arsenal did in the Premier League in 2003-4.

In 1889, PNE won the league as well as the FA Cup, and managed not to concede a single goal in the tournament.

They didn't have one specific manager, but instead had a committee whose job it was to select the players. PNE played in a 2-3-5 formation, which was popular at the time, and used their players very cleverly.

DICK, KERR LADIES, UK
1917–25

During World War I, at the Preston branch of a locomotive and tramcar manufacturer called Dick, Kerr & Co., female employees started playing in their breaks, and they became incredibly good.

In 1917, Dick, Kerr Ladies played the factory's men's team and won. In 1920, they played against St Helen's Ladies in front of 53,000 people.

In 1922, Dick, Kerr Ladies toured North America. They played nine men's teams, winning three matches and drawing three. The men's teams included professional players and future USA national team players.

HUNGARY NATIONAL TEAM
1950–56

Also known as the Mighty Magyars or the Golden Team, the Hungary national team played 50 games over six years and lost only one of them, to West Germany in the 1954 World Cup final.

They were managed by Gusztáv Sebes, and their best player was Ferenc Puskás. The Puskás Award for the most impressive goal of the season in world football is named after him.

The Magyars won gold in the 1952 Olympics and beat England 6-3 at Wembley in what became known as the Match of the Century a year later. They scored in 73 consecutive games, which is still a record. The Golden Team indeed!

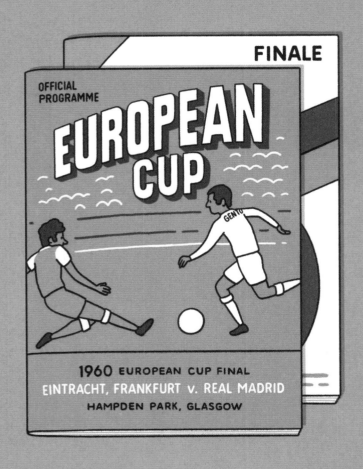

REAL MADRID, SPAIN
1955–60

This Real Madrid team were the original Galácticos (superstars). There were stars in every position on the pitch, but the best were Francisco Gento (left-wing), Raymond Kopa (right-wing), Alfredo Di Stéfano (centre-forward) and Ferenc Puskás (centre-forward or inside forward).

The legendary Di Stéfano would often drop back into the midfield, which meant that this Real Madrid side could switch easily from a 3-2-5 formation to a 3-2-2-3 formation, which was confusing to their opponents!

The original Galácticos won five European Cups (Champions Leagues) in a row. This had never been done before and has never been done since.

AJAX, NETHERLANDS
1970-73

This Ajax side were coached by Rinus Michels, who became a very influential football manager. In 1970, Michels taught his players about Total Football. He wanted every player to be able to play every position, so if you noticed your teammate was out of position, you would be able to step in.

Ajax were close to relegation when Michels took over, but he turned them into world-beaters.

Michels left for Barcelona in 1971 and was replaced by Stefán Kovács. It was down to Kovács and Ajax hero Johan Cruyff that they won three European Cups in a row.

GERMANY WOMEN'S NATIONAL TEAM
1989-2008

This was one of the most successful international football teams of all time. In German, they are called the Deutsche Fußballnationalmannschaft der Frauen, and they had a winning spree between their first European Championships win in 1989 and their World Cup win in 2007.

They have won eight of the 12 European Championships so far, and claimed six consecutive titles between 1995 and 2013. They also won the World Cup in 2003 and claimed Olympic bronze in 2000, 2004 and 2008. Superstar Birgit Prinz scored 128 goals in 214 appearances. It is fair to say they have won the lot.

FINALE EUROPA CUP
WOENSDAG 31 MEI 1972
INTERNAZIONALE v AJAX
STADION ROTTERDAM FEYENOORD
RINUS MICHELS

BARCELONA 2008–11 & SPAIN 2008–12

These two sides played a style of football called tiki-taka. This is a technique where players make lots of little passes without letting the other side touch the ball. These teams shared many of the same players and dominated European football for four years.

Barcelona were so good at keeping the ball that if you wanted to touch the ball when you were up against them, it was probably just better to bring your own ball from home and do keepie-uppies in the corner until the game was over.

For those four years, it seemed as though players such as Messi, Xavi, Iniesta and Busquets could not be beaten, until the rest of the world figured out how to play in the same way.

Spain won the Euros in 2008 and 2012, and the World Cup in 2010. Barcelona won La Liga in 2009, 2010 and 2011, as well as the treble in 2009 of La Liga, Copa del Rey and Champions League. Barcelona won the Champions League again in 2011 and are considered by many to be the greatest football team of all time.

OLYMPIQUE LYONNAIS FÉMININ, FRANCE
2007–19

Lyon's women's team are the most dominant football team of all time. With star players such as England's Lucy Bronze, Wendie Renard, Amandine Henry, legendary striker Eugénie Le Sommer and the Ballon d'Or-winning Ada Hegerberg, Lyon have been simply amazing.

Since 2010, Lyon have won six Champions League titles, four of them coming consecutively between 2016 and 2019, as well as 13 consecutive French Ligue 1s from 2007 to 2019. This sort of domination may never be seen again in football anywhere in the world.

REAL MADRID, SPAIN
2016–18

With Madrid hero Zinedine Zidane, nicknamed 'Zizou', as the manager, the team won three Champions Leagues in a row, something that hadn't happened for over 40 years.

Zizou took over from Rafa Benítez at Real Madrid in 2016. This was controversial as Rafa had only lost three games in his time as manager. However, Zizou went on to dominate the Champions League with Real Madrid just as he had done as a player. If anyone was going to get the best out of Real Madrid's megastars, it makes sense that it was Zizou, the ultimate Galáctico.

USA WOMEN'S NATIONAL TEAM
1991 – PRESENT

Since winning that first World Cup in 1991, the USA went on to win the competition again in 1999, 2015 and 2019. Alongside the World Cup success came Olympic gold medals in 1996, 2004, 2008 and 2012. That's a lot of trophies and gold medals. They've won the CONCACAF Cup eight times, the Algarve Cup ten times and two of the first four She Believes Cups since it began in 2016. They have been unstoppable.

Many of the greatest women ever to play the game have represented the USA, including their top three goalscorers of all time: Abby Wambach (184 goals), Mia Hamm (158 goals) and Kristine Lilly (130 goals).

FOOTBALL BOOTS PAST TO PRESENT

Do you have a favourite pair of football boots? Nowadays, football boots are super high-tech tools, every tiny detail designed to help players run and kick perfectly and, of course, to look cool. It took a long time to get to this point. The amazing Predators or Vapors you have on your feet today are very different from the soggy leather clogs that our footballing ancestors were wearing. Let's take a look at the evolution of the boot...

1800s

In the 1800s, if you wanted to play football, you played in your work boots. They were thick, heavy leather boots. The leather went up past your ankles and, in the rain, they could weigh a kilo. They often had steel toecaps. Imagine getting a steel kick in a tackle. Ouch!

1990s

The 1990s saw the release of the iconic adidas Predators. Predators had rubber ridges where you were most likely to strike the ball, helping you to 'grip' it and add curve to your shots. Predators have evolved over time to the ultra high-tech engineered version we see now. Zidane scored one of the greatest goals of all time in the 2002 Champions League final wearing Predator Manias.

1994

Nike brought out the Tiempo Premiers for the 1994 World Cup in the USA. The Nike Tiempo has been a popular boot since then, with players such as Ronaldinho, Andrea Pirlo, and Francesco Totti all being extremely good at football while wearing them.

1998

Nike created the Mercurial boot in 1998. They were silver, blue, yellow and swirly. They were lighter than most boots. Ronaldo had a special pair that Nike called the 'R9's. In 2002, the Mercurials evolved into the timeless Mercurial Vapors.

Thierry Daniel Henry was a forward who played for Monaco, Juventus, Barcelona, New York Red Bulls and, most famously, Arsenal. Premier League defences were used to dealing with powerful forwards who acted as target men. Henry caused havoc in his Mercurial Vapors.

1954

In 1954, a German called Adi Dassler created a new type of football boot. You guessed it; this was the beginning of adidas. Adi Dassler designed screw-in studs that could be attached to your boots, giving you better grip on rainy, muddy surfaces.

1970s

In the 1970s, Alan Ball became the first player to wear white boots. Ball was famous for winning the World Cup with England in 1966. His boots were designed by Hummel, and they were so bright that the commentator called him 'Twinkle Toes'.

1980s

Puma released the Puma King in the 1980s, and they became a competitor to the Copa Mundial. Puma Kings were worn by players such as Diego Maradona and Johan Cruyff, while Alan Shearer scored hundreds of goals in the new Umbro boots.

1979

In 1979, adidas released the Copa Mundial. They had big tongues to cover the laces. Tongues were popular because covering the laces was thought to help players strike more accurately. The Copa Mundials were simple, durable and comfy. They are the best-selling boot of all time.

2010

The 2010s saw a return to the ankle collar. This time they were for comfort rather than protection. Modern boots are also often laceless to help shooting accuracy. No fancy boot helps as much as simply practising a lot. Modern boots are amazing, but striker Sergio Agüero could play in wellies and he'd still score goals for fun.

Jackie Milburn is a Newcastle United legend who complained that the new boots were too light. Jackie wanted heavy, durable boots. He would wear his sturdy football boots in the bath, or when he was working in the mines, so that they would mould to his feet.

Blades started to replace studs in the late '90s, as they provided better grip. But, by the end of the '00s, they'd dipped in popularity as they gave so much grip on the pitch that players began twisting their ankles and complaining of injuries.

THE EVOLUTION OF THE BALL

The ball. The most important thing of all! Without the football there'd be no last-minute wonder-goals, no last-ditch headers, no... well, nothing really. The ball has changed a lot from its humble beginnings as anything sort-of round to the sleek and perfected ball we have now.

Remember Ts'u-chü, the Chinese game that used a leather ball stuffed with animal hair and feathers? Well, that isn't the strangest ball in history...

It is believed that in South America, hundreds of years ago, football was often played using ...

... A HUMAN HEAD! A long time ago, in South America, if you committed a particularly terrible crime, you would be beheaded and your head could be used as a football. Does that mean every goal was technically a header?

Thankfully, things changed.

Don't worry if you don't have a top-of-the-range football. The Brazilian hero, Pelé, grew up playing with a bunch of rolled-up socks instead of a ball, and he went on to be one of the greatest players of all time.

In the 1800s, most footballs were made from pig bladders. Not all pig bladders are the same size, which meant neither were footballs. It was in the late 1800s when the FA decided that all balls used in their competitions must be roughly the same size and weight. This meant that a new way of making footballs had to be found.

In the first official World Cup Final between Uruguay and Argentina in 1930, both teams used their own footballs instead of a neutral ball provided by FIFA. In the first half, Argentina used their own football, and they were 2-1 up at half time. Uruguay used their ball in the second half and went on to win the game 4-2.

The ball used for the 2018 World Cup in Russia was a modern version of the adidas Telstar. It was black and white, just like the original Telstar.

Benjamin Pavard scored the best goal of the 2018 World Cup with the adidas Telstar 18. It was a totally ridiculous, rising volley from outside the area. France were losing 2-1 at the time, and went on to win 4-3.

At the 2010 World Cup, the Jabulani ball was released. It had just eight panels which made it incredibly smooth. This made the ball move about unpredictably in the air. Strikers and goalkeepers complained, as nobody knew what was going to happen to the ball after it had been kicked. It was chaotic, but very exciting.

For the 2006 World Cup in Germany, adidas introduced the Teamgeist football. It had 14 panels instead of the 32 in the Buckminster design. This made it smoother and more streamlined. Being streamlined means that the shape of something helps it to move faster through the air.

The first non-black-and-white official ball was used at the 1998 World Cup in France. The ball was white with blue and red details – the same colours as the French flag – and was named the Tricolore.

In 1951, the first ever white-and-orange footballs were allowed in competitive games, to aid visibility in bad weather. Previously, all balls were brown.

In 1970, the first official World Cup ball was produced: the adidas Telstar. This is what most people imagine when they think of a football. The black-and-white design was created by Richard Buckminster Fuller and is called The Buckminster Design.

BRAZIL 1970 WORLD CUP FINAL GOAL

Brazilian right wing-back Carlos Alberto scored one of the greatest World Cup goals ever with the adidas Telstar in the 1970 final against Italy. Pelé set him up. Nice.

THE GREAT PLAYERS

From year to year, season to season, week to week and even from day to day, different players fall in and out of favour for all sorts of reasons. It can seem impossible to keep up. However, there are some players from history who are indisputable legends. Players who were heads, shoulders, knees and toes above everyone else playing around them. We've chosen 11 of the greatest for you to read about, dream about and learn from.

BORN: 26th June 1968, Milan, Italy

PLAYED FOR: 906 appearances for A.C. Milan between 1984 and 2009, 126 appearances for Italy.

WHAT THEY SAID ABOUT PAOLO: Italian striker Alessandro Del Piero said, 'There are great players and there are world-class players. Then there are those who manage to go beyond that term. Paolo is the perfect example'.

FACT: His dad, Cesare, also played for A.C. Milan and also won the Champions League with them as captain, 40 years before Paolo did.

Maldini was a magnificent defender because he could do everything. He was a dogged marker, a graceful passer, an elegant dribbler, a fantastic crosser and a precise tackler. He was a very intelligent footballer with unrivalled tactical awareness and knowledge. He also taught himself to kick equally well with either foot.

All of this meant that Maldini could play in any defensive position: left, right, centre, wing back, wherever. With A.C. Milan, he won 7 Serie A titles and 5 Champions Leagues. He won the lot, did Paolo, and had gorgeous hair to go with it.

PAOLO MALDINI
DEFENDER

GOALKEEPER

LEV YASHIN

BORN: 22nd October 1929, Moscow, Russia

PLAYED FOR: 326 appearances for Dynamo Moscow from 1950 to 1970, 74 appearances for the Soviet Union.

WHAT THEY SAID ABOUT LEV: Portuguese legend Eusebio called him 'the peerless goalkeeper of the century'.

FACT: Also played international ice hockey. He was a goalkeeper in this sport, too.

Lev Yashin was born in the Soviet Union (now Russia) and was in their World Cup squad four times. He was known as 'The Black Spider' because of his kit and because he made so many saves it was as though he had eight legs.

His clothes weren't actually black, they were dark blue, but on the black-and-white TVs of the time, his clothes looked black to the people watching.

He was incredibly acrobatic and had a reputation for putting strikers off just by being so scary. He saved 150 penalties and kept 270 clean sheets and is the only goalkeeper ever to win the Ballon d'Or (the award for the best player in the world).

DEFENDER
JOY FAWCETT

DEFENDER

FRANZ BECKENBAUER

BORN: 8th February 1968, California, USA

PLAYED FOR: 43 appearances for San Diego Spirit, 241 appearances for USA national team between 1987 and 2004.

WHAT THEY SAID ABOUT JOY: The USA Women's Team Hall of Fame said, 'Her innate ability to read the game, to defuse potential danger before it became dangerous, was one of her greatest and always overlooked talents'.

FACT: Currently assistant coach for USA Women's Deaf Team.

Fawcett was tenacious, tough and extremely clever. She won the first ever Women's World Cup with the USA in China, 1991, and went on to win 241 caps for the USA.

She had children while she was still a player, came back to the sport immediately after they were born and played as if she'd never been away. Having a baby is probably one of the most difficult things a human can do, but Fawcett did it and then just immediately started giving opposition attackers nightmares again. She then went on to become a founding member of the WUSA.

BORN: 11th September 1945, Munich, Germany

PLAYED FOR: 439 appearances for Bayern Munich, 105 for New York Cosmos, 28 for Hamburger SV, 103 for West Germany.

WHAT THEY SAID ABOUT FRANZ: Brian Clough, European Cup-winning manager with Nottingham Forest, remembered that he 'once saw Franz Beckenbauer enter a restaurant and he did it the same way he played football: with class and authority'.

FACT: The first player to win the World Cup, European Championships and European Cup (Champions League) all as captain.

Franz Beckenbauer invented a position. Beckenbauer was the first attacking sweeper, or libero. He was a rock-solid defender but he was also very comfortable on the ball. He would win the ball back from the opposition, then run with it all the way to the other end of the field and create attacking opportunities for his team. He did the job of three or four players on his own.

He was known as Der Kaiser, which means 'The Emperor' in German.

JOHAN CRUYFF

MIDFIELDER

BORN: 25th April 1947, Amsterdam, Netherlands

PLAYED FOR: 273 appearances for Ajax, 143 for Barcelona, 23 for Los Angeles Aztecs, 30 for Washington Diplomats, 10 for Levante, 33 for Feyenoord.

WHAT THEY SAID ABOUT JOHAN: Dutch player Johan Neeskens said, 'If you look at the greatest players in history, most of them couldn't coach. If you look at the greatest coaches in history, most of them were not great players. Johan Cruyff did both – and in such an exhilarating style'.

FACT: He invented a whole style of football called 'Total Football'.

Johan Cruyff is labelled as a midfielder here, but he could play in any position (except maybe goalkeeper).

Cruyff was a huge believer in 'total football', which is the idea that every outfield player on the pitch should be able to play in

BORN: 1st February 1966, California, USA

PLAYED FOR: Tyresö FF, Orlando Lions Women, 155 appearances for the USA national team between 1985 and 200.

WHAT THEY SAID ABOUT MICHELLE: Mia Hamm, fellow USA national team player, said, 'If it's a header, I'm putting all my money, and all the other team's money, on Michelle'.

FACT: She started playing as a striker, and was probably the best player in the world. She scored in almost every game she played. She won the Golden Boot for most goals scored at the 1991 World Cup in China, and won with the USA.

After the World Cup she started feeling constantly exhausted and was told she had chronic fatigue and immune dysfunction syndrome, which made her feel tired all the time.

She could have stopped playing after that but she didn't. She played as a defensive midfielder instead, a position in which she didn't need to sprint as much.

She went on to win the World Cup again with the USA in 1999. All hail Queen Akers!

MICHELLE AKERS
MIDFIELDER

every position. So if he noticed that a right-back player went sprinting up the pitch to help the attack, he would just fill in the space the right-back had left while somebody else filled his position and so on. (Read more about positions on p.34)

Cruyff won eight Eredivisie (the top Dutch League) titles with Ajax. He played in this Total Football style at Barcelona, too. In 1974 he helped Barcelona to win their first Liga (the top Spanish League) since 1960. He won three Ballons d'Or and helped to change the way football is played.

Cruyff also invented an astonishing and signature move called the Cruyff Turn. He would feign a pass mid-dribble and then turn and speed-off in the opposite direction. Pep Guardiola was a student of Johan Cruyff and shares a lot of the same tactical ideas.

ZINEDINE ZIDANE
MIDFIELDER

BORN: 23rd June 1972, Marseille, France

PLAYED FOR: 61 appearances for Cannes, 139 for Bordeaux, 151 for Juventus, 155 for Real Madrid, 108 for France.

WHAT THEY SAID ABOUT ZIZOU: Zlatan Ibrahimović said, 'When Zidane stepped onto the pitch, the 10 other guys just got suddenly better. It was magic. He was a unique player. He was more than good, he came from another planet. His teammates became like him when he was on the pitch'.

FACT: Got sent off in the 2010 World Cup final, his last ever match.

Known by his teammates as Zizou, he moved around the pitch like a dancer, with elegance and grace. He could shoot equally well with either foot, and he was the master of the 'roulette', a skill move that involves spinning past your opponent like a ballet dancer.

He scored one of the greatest ever Champions League goals for Real Madrid in the final against Leverkusen in 2002. The ball was hooked high into the sky by Roberto Carlos, and as it fell, Zizou never took his eyes off it, opened up his body and smashed a volley into the top corner with his ever-so-slightly weaker left foot. Zizou won the Italian Serie A twice, La Liga once, the Champions League once, and the World Cup in France. He scored two headers in the World Cup final in 1998 with his lovely, shiny skull.

SIR STANLEY MATTHEWS
MIDFIELDER

MARTA VIEIRA DA SILVA
ATTACKER

BORN: 1st February 1915, Stoke-on-Trent, UK

PLAYED FOR: 355 appearances for Stoke City, 428 for Blackpool, 54 for England.

WHAT THEY SAID ABOUT STANLEY:
Gianfranco Zola, a former Chelsea and Italy player, said, 'Stanley told me he used to play for just £20 a week. Today he would be worth all the money in the Bank of England.'

FACT: Despite the horrendous apartheid laws (which meant black people were not given the same rights as white people) in place in South Africa at the time, Stanley Matthews travelled to Soweto in 1975 and set up an all-black youth team in the area. He coached young South Africans of all races for years afterwards.

Known as 'The Wizard of the Dribble', Matthews played as a winger and ran with the ball unlike anybody else at the time. He won the first ever Ballon d'Or in 1956, and was so fit that he played until he was 50 years old in the top division in England, which is a record to this day. Matthews won the FA Cup with Blackpool in 1953.

BORN: 19th February 1986, Alagoas, Brazil

PLAYED FOR: 16 appearances at Vasco da Gama, 103 for Umeå IK, 24 for FC Gold Pride, 49 for Orlando Pride, 147 for Brazil.

WHAT MARTA SAID: After being knocked out of the World Cup in 2019, Marta said, 'The women's game depends on you to survive. So think about that. Value it more. Cry in the beginning so you can smile in the end'.

FACT: Her 17 goals at World Cup finals cemented her position as top World Cup goal scorer of all time.

Marta is often referred to as the greatest female footballer of all time, and with good reason. Her dribbling skills are second to none.

She's incredibly fast and has scored an impressive number of goals despite not always playing as a striker.

BORN: 23rd October 1940, Minas Gerais, Brazil

PLAYED FOR: 656 (1,120 including friendlies) appearances for Santos, 107 for NY Cosmos, 92 for Brazil.

WHAT THEY SAID ABOUT PELÉ: Former Manchester United striker Eric Cantona said that Pelé was 'an artist in my eyes, someone who can lighten up a dark room'.

FACT: As a child, Pele used to practise with a newspaper rolled up into a ball with a piece of string attached to it.

For a long time, Pelé was considered to be the greatest football player of all time, and he still is by some. He played as a striker or as an attacking midfielder and had many fantastic skills, but his main talent was scoring goals. Pelé scored 1,283 goals in 1,366 matches.

Pelé was named the FIFA Player of the Century for the 20th Century. He won three World Cups with Brazil and two Copa Libertadores with Santos.

EDSON ARANTES DO NASCIMENTO

AKA **PELÉ**

ATTACKER

37

LIONEL MESSI

ACKER

BORN: 24th June 1987, Rosario, Argentina

PLAYED FOR: Newell's Old Boys before moving to Barcelona, for whom he has made 687 appearances.

WHAT THEY SAID ABOUT MESSI: Ex-teammate at Barcelona Javier Mascherano said, 'Although he may not be human, it's good that Messi still thinks he is'.

Messi plays football at a different level from everyone else. He is arguably the greatest football player there has ever been. He is one of the most impressive finishers, passers, free-kick takers and dribblers of all time. He also has a sixth sense when it comes to the sport. He knows the perfect place to stand, exactly when to run, the right moment to pass and the precise angle at which to shoot. Sometimes skill like this can't be taught and instead it should just be admired.

LEGENDARY MANAGERS
AND HOW THEY DID IT

Football management is difficult. Imagine having to tell 11 people on a big pitch where to stand while you have a bench of subs next to you who all think they should be playing, and 50,000 people in a crowd who, really, think they should be playing too. But it's also super rewarding. Winning trophies for your players, your club and your fans must be the most amazing feeling in the world. And to do so you have to be pretty brainy. Not in a way that means you finish top in the class at everything, just in a way that means you have your own ideas and act on them. And when your own ideas are going wrong, you are flexible enough to change them.

Here are those managers who changed the way football was played forever, and some examples of the formations they played and why.

THE KEY POSITIONS

Where you play on the field is not just random. You probably have something you are particularly good at: maybe you run fast, maybe you are tall, maybe you like to think up clever tactics and maybe you have a knack for smashing in goals. Whatever it is, there is a position for you. The job of a manager is to choose which players they think will work best in which position and match their special skills to work well with the rest of the team. Here are the key positions as well as some slightly more specialist ones.

GOALKEEPER

The goalie is the only player allowed to use their hands, and with that comes a lot of responsibility. Their main job is to stop the ball from going into the net. They need good concentration, to be agile, to have good reactions and increasingly, they need to be able to pass the ball well.

FULL BACK

There are usually two full back players, a left back and a right back. They go on the sides of the defence, either side of the centre backs. They need to be quick and good at changing direction as opposition 'wingers' will try to dribble past them to get closer to the penalty area, or to the edge of the area to put in a cross. Increasingly, full backs are often expected to link up attacks and even score goals themselves.

CENTRE BACK

The centre back, sometimes known as a centre-half, is the player in the middle of the defence. Their main job is to stop the opposition from getting any chances to have a shot at goal. They're usually big – normally the biggest on the pitch. They also have to be strong, able to read the game, to intercept opposition passes and predict them before they happen, and also be very brave.

CENTRE MIDFIELD

Often referred to as the 'Engine of the Team', a centre midfielder needs many qualities. They're in the middle of the pitch and will need to be able to win headers and tackles, make interceptions, start attacks, play long balls and indeed score goals. They are busy bees.

STRIKER

The striker's main job is to score goals. Strikers come in all shapes and sizes, but generally have one outstanding quality: they are good at finishing.

DEFENSIVE MIDFIELD

Similar to the centre midfielder, but the
defensive midfielder plays deeper, just in front
of the defence. Claude Makélélé was possibly
the best ever at this: identifying attacks and
stopping them before they could get going. In
fact, he was so good that people often refer to
this position as the 'Makélélé' role.

WINGER

The winger's job is to create and score goals,
usually by starting wide and taking on the
opposition's full back with skill and pace.
Traditionally, a winger would get to the bye-
line and put in a cross, but a winger's job has
evolved more to getting into the penalty area,
cutting in and scoring goals themselves.

WING BACK

A wing back will usually play in a
'Back Five': a formation that has
three centre backs and two wing
backs. They play down the sides –
the wings – of the pitch, like a full
back, but are expected to move
up and down the pitch more. They
have to be amazingly fit to do this.

TREQUARTISTA
OR NUMBER 10

They play ahead of the
midfield but behind the
strikers. They are imaginative
and skilful – Argentinian
Diego Maradona could be
considered a trequartista.

LIBERO OR SWEEPER

They go behind the two centre backs and
sweep up the danger. They are strong and
can read the game like a book.

UTILITY PLAYER

A player who doesn't have a specific
position and can slot in where necessary.
James Milner is a good example: he's
great all over the pitch.

MANAGERS AND FORMATIONS

Most teams who win anything have a good manager behind them. Lots of managers are reliable and effective, but some managers are absolute game changers in the truest sense of the word. They invent formations, which means they plan where each player is positioned on the pitch. Formations are often a manager's trademark and key to their success. Here are a few of the best, along with their favourite killer formations and most innovative tactics.

RINUS MICHELS

Marinus Jacobus Hendricus Michels is the wise owl of football managers. Michels invented the version of 'Total Football' that is commonly referred to in modern football. You don't get named FIFA Coach of the Century for nothing. He inspired many managers who followed, including Johan Cruyff and Pep Guardiola, who you are about to meet.

As a coach, Michels won the European Cup, the European Championship, four Eredivisies, three KNVB Cups, La Liga and the Copa del Rey.

TOTAL FOOTBALL

Every player in the team should be capable of playing any position on the pitch.

Players have to be very versatile and responsive. Only versatile players can play Total Football.

If a player leaves their position, another player takes up the empty space so that all the positions are covered at any given time. Pep Guardiola's Manchester City do this well.

The lineage of Total Football is traceable throughout time. Michels coached Cruyff and Cruyff coached Guardiola.

JOHAN CRUYFF

Johan Cruyff is thought to be the most influential man in football from the past 50 years, if not of all time. He was coached by Michels and took Total Football even further.

Cruyff made sure that the youth, reserve and first teams at his clubs played the same tactics so that it was easier to promote youth players to the first team. He created the training exercise called 'rondos'. Rondos is a bit like piggy-in-the-middle with a football. It helps develop players' spatial awareness.

Ajax's youth academy is based on Cruyff's football philosophy. He also helped to establish the famous Barcelona youth academy, La Masia. La Masia teaches players to be humble and unselfish so that they can learn more. Many of the best players of the past two decades were educated at La Masia. In 2012, Barcelona played a team made up entirely of La Masia graduates: Víctor Valdés, Jordi Alba, Carles Puyol, Gerard Piqué, Martín Montoya, Sergio Busquets, Xavi, Andrés Iniesta, Cesc Fàbregas, Pedro and Lionel Messi.

Cruyff's Barcelona won La Liga four times in a row, as well as the 1992 Champions League, after which a million people lined the streets of Barcelona to celebrate their return. Cruyff is also famous for having fantastic hair.

PEP GUARDIOLA

Josep 'Pep' Guardiola played under the management of Johan Cruyff and Bobby Robson at Barcelona.

In his first season as Barcelona manager, he won the first ever treble in Spanish football and became the youngest manager to win the Champions League.

Pep and Manchester City became the first manager and team to earn 100 points in a Premier League season and the first English men's team to complete a domestic treble (FA Cup, League Cup and Premier League).

Pep invented a formation tactic called 'the false 9'. He instructed Lionel Messi to play in the centre of the attack, but also to drop deep and look for the ball. Guardiola is also responsible for making goalkeepers more comfortable on the ball. This is because his tactics require goalkeepers to play the ball out from the back and act as an extra outfield player.

Pressing is the word used to describe when a team rushes at the opposition in order to limit their time on the ball, as opposed to sitting back and waiting for the opposition to attack.

VALERIY LOBANOVSKYI

Not all managers make it big through formations and tactics alone. Lobanovskyi was one of the first coaches to place importance on the fitness and diet of his players.

He won the second most trophies of any manager ever, after Alex Ferguson, winning 13 league titles in Ukraine and the Soviet Union, nine cups in the same countries, two Cup Winners Cups and one European Super Cup.

He also managed to steer Dynamo Kyiv to the semi finals of the 1999 Champions League among some incredible competition from English, Spanish, German and Italian sides.

BOB PAISLEY

Bob Paisley was born in Hetton-le-Hole, played for Bishop Auckland and then made the move directly to Liverpool, which is quite a jump. As a manager, Bob was given the task of following on from the legendary Bill Shankly, who had become a hero at Anfield (Liverpool's stadium).

Paisley was in charge of Liverpool for nine years, winning nothing in his first year. After that first year, though, he won at least one major trophy in every year of his time at Liverpool, including six league titles, three European Cups and the UEFA Cup! Only two other managers have won three Champions League: Zinedine Zidane and Carlo Ancelotti.

Paisley's teams would mainly play a 4-4-2 formation. This was one of the most popular formations for most of the 1980s and is still used by many teams today. Two lines of four players in midfield and defence is difficult to break down, while counter-attacking is made possible with two central strikers forming a partnership.

SIR ALEX FERGUSON

Sir Alexander Chapman Ferguson, or Fergie, is the most successful Manchester United manager. At the young age of 32, he started his managerial career at East Stirlingshire, with whom he started winning league titles.

He moved to Manchester United in 1986. It took him until 1993 to win the league, although he did win the FA Cup and the League Cup in the meantime. When three of United's best players, Hughes, Ince and Kanchelskis, left the club in 1995, people lost confidence in Fergie. He chose six very young inexperienced players from the youth setup. They were Gary and Phil Neville, David Beckham, Nicky Butt, Paul Scholes and Ryan Giggs. They all turned out to be superstars and became known as the class of '92. Sir Alex coined the phrase 'squeaky bum time', meaning when things get tense towards the end of a match or season.

Sir Alex liked a few different formations, including 4-2-3-1. In this formation, the midfield is very full. This means that the opponents find it hard to command space in the middle and may have to resort to playing risky long balls.

CORINNE DIACRE

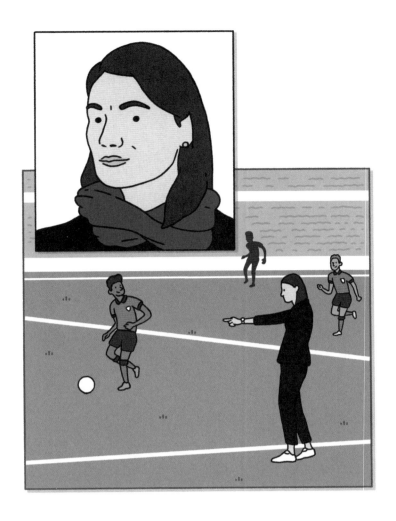

Corinne Diacre began her career as a defender. She played for the French national side making 121 appearances. In August 2014, Diacre became the first woman to manage a men's football team, Clermont Foot. This was a huge step for women in the sport and a testament to her sheer tactical brilliance and insight in the sport.

She is now the manager of the French women's national team, which features many players from the very successful Lyon squad.

CHAN YUEN TING

Chan Yuen Ting was born in Hong Kong in 1988. In 2016 she won the Hong Kong Premier League as manager of the men's team, Eastern Sports Club.

It is very rare for a professional coach or manager to be this young because it can be difficult to lead a team where most of the players are older. Chan Yuen Ting did not let this faze her and took her men's team to victory, winning in Hong Kong's top division when she was only 27. She became the first female football manager to win a men's top division in international history. She has helped to increase the popularity of the Hong Kong Premier League.

Her favourite formation is 4-3-3, which is one of the most popular formations in football right now. It was used by the famous Dutch, Ajax and Barcelona teams who played Total Football.

THE BIG CUPS

Across the world, in every country there are football leagues of every quality. A league is a set of teams of a similar standard. Within a season, each team within a league will play every other team a certain number of times (usually twice: home and away). Each match has points ascribed to it, and the team that wins the most points on the league table wins the league.

A cup competition is slightly different from a league. Cup competitions usually involve knock-out games, meaning that if a team loses, they leave the competition. Occasionally there are group stages to a cup competition, which means there are mini leagues, followed by a knock-out final stage.

The international cups are arguably the most dramatic competitions. They tend to be the biggest, most watched and most special to the teams who win them.

WORLD CUP (MEN'S)

To a football fan, the World Cup is like a birthday, but if a birthday came around every four years and lasted for a whole month. It's the biggest, most exciting, most colourful festival of sport in the world. It features the best national teams from around the world and for the month that it runs, the entire globe seems to catch football fever.

Started by a man called Jules Rimet, the first World Cup took place in 1930 in Uruguay. Thirteen teams took part and Uruguay were victorious. Since then seven other countries have won titles: Brazil have five (1958, 1962, 1970, 1994, 2002), Italy have four (1934, 1938, 1982, 2006), Germany have four (1954, 1974, 1990, 2014), Argentina have two (1978, 1986), France have two (1998, 2018), England have one (1966) and Spain have one (2010). Uruguay won once more in 1950, when they beat the host country Brazil, at the Estádio do Maracanã in Rio de Janeiro, 2-1. Over 199,000 watched the nail-biting match.

One of the most famous goals was scored at the Mexico 1986 World Cup. Diego Maradona headed in an unlikely and impressive goal for Argentina against England that some people felt was a handball. When interviewed about it he said he had scored it 'a little with my head, and a little with the hand of God'. Argentina went on to win the cup.

WORLD CUP (WOMEN'S)

Historically, women's football has not been given the attention it deserves. The Women's World Cup didn't officially start until 1991, 61 years after the men's. The first tournament was officially called the FIFA World Championship for Women's Football for the M&M's Cup. The United States won it and their star player, Michelle Akers was the top scorer with ten goals. That's four more goals than Harry Kane scored at the 2018 World Cup!

The USA have won the World Cup four times, Germany have won it twice, and Japan and Norway have won one each.

At the 2019 World Cup in France, legendary Brazil striker Marta Vieira da Silva gave a rallying speech to young and aspiring female footballers after her side were knocked out of the competition by tournament hosts France.

'Women's football depends on you to survive. Think about it, value it more. We're asking for support, you have to cry at the beginning and smile at the end. It's about wanting more, it's about training more, it's about looking after yourself more, it's about being ready to play 90 minutes and then 30 minutes more. So that's why I am asking the girls. There's not going to be a Formiga forever, there's not going to be a Marta forever, there's not going to be a Cristiane.'

EUROPEAN CHAMPIONSHIPS

Also known as the Euros, this international tournament began in 1960 and features national teams from all over Europe. The Euros, just like the World Cup, are played every four years. They can be hosted by a single country or by lots at once, with the 2020 Euros being played all across Europe. The most successful teams in the Euros have been Spain and Germany, each winning it three times. Spain won the tournament twice in a row with their brilliant tiki-taka technique and Barcelona-heavy teams of 2008 and 2012 (see p.17).

AFRICAN CUP OF NATIONS

Shortened to 'AFCON', the African Cup of Nations has been running since 1957 when only three national teams took part: Sudan, Egypt and Ethiopia. Now, 24 national teams compete in the tournament, which usually takes place every two years. There have been 16 winners at AFCON: Egypt, United Arab Republic, Ethiopia, Ghana, Congo-Kinshasha, Sudan, Congo, Zaire, Morocco, Nigeria, Cameroon, Algeria, Ivory Coast, South Africa, Tunisia and Zambia.

The Ghanaian player Abédi 'Pelé' Ayew was crowned player of the tournament at the 1992 AFCON, hosted by Senegal. Abédi played for French team Olympique de Marseille and the following year would go on to win the European Cup with them, helping them to become the only French club to ever win the competition. Abédi has three sons – Ibrahim, André and Jordan – who are all professional footballers… and have all played for Ghana.

OLYMPIC GAMES

Since 1900, men's football has been a sport in the Olympic Games. Only amateur teams and, with the exception of three players, under-23-year-old players are allowed to play in the men's tournament. Women's football has featured since 1996.

THE AFC ASIAN CUP

This cup is played by national teams from across Asia. This cup has been held every four years since 1956, although after the 2004 cup it was brought forward a year to stop it from clashing with the Summer Olympics and the Euros. Japan are the most successful team, with four tournament victories, with Saudi Arabia and Iraq in joint-second, having won three each.

COPA AMÉRICA

The oldest men's international tournament in the world, the Copa América features national teams from South America, and since 1993, teams from Asia and North America, too. Uruguay won the first competition in 1916, and have gone on to become its most successful team, winning 15 in total.

1 LIGUE 1

Location: France
Founded: 1930
Most Titles: Saint-Étienne (10)
Top Goalscorer: Delio Onnis - 299
A big moment: Between
2002-8, Olympique Lyonnais
won seven titles in a row.

2 NWSL

Location: USA
Founded: 2012 (after Women's Professional
Soccer in 2007 and Women's United Soccer
Association in 2001)
Most Titles: FC Kansas City and Portland
Thorns FC (2)
Top Goalscorer: Samantha Kerr - 64
A big moment: In 2002, Michelle Akers, who
started at University team UCF Knights, wins
FIFA Female Player of the Century.

3 LA LIGA

Location: Spain
Founded: 1929
Most Titles: Real Madrid (33)
Top Goalscorer: Lionel Messi - 419,
and counting
A big moment: In 2009, Barcelona
became the first Spanish team to win the
treble of La Liga, the Copa del Rey, and the
Champions League.

4 FAWSL

Location: England
Founded: 2010 (formerly FA Women's
National League, founded in 1992)
Most Titles: Arsenal (3)
Top Goalscorer: Nikita Parris - 37
A big moment: Vivianne Miedema scored
22 goals for Arsenal during the 2018/19
season, seven more than any previous top

5 SERIE A

Location: Italy
Founded: 1898
Most Titles: Juventus (35)
Top Goalscorer: Silvio Piola - 274
A big moment: In 1987, Diego
Maradona arrived in Naples and led
them to their first ever league title.

6 DIVISION 1 FÉMININE

Location: France
Founded: 1974
Most Titles: Olympique Lyonnais (17)
Top Goalscorer: Ada Hegerberg - 130
A big moment: Since 2007, Olympique
Lyonnais have won the league every
single year.

7 J-LEAGUE

Location: Japan
Founded: 1992
Most Titles: Kashima Antlers (8)
Top Goalscorer: Yoshito Ōkubo - 179
A big moment: Dutch striker Henny
Meijer scored the league's first ever goal
for Tokyo Verdy.

8 CHINESE SUPER LEAGUE

Location: China
Founded: 2004
Most Titles: Guangzhou Evergrande Taobao (7)
Top Goalscorer: Wu Lei - 102, and counting
A big moment: The World Cup-winning Italian
coach Marcello Lippi led Guangzhou Evergrande
Taobao to three titles in a row between 2012-14.

9 MLS

Location: USA and Canada
Founded: 1993
Most Titles: LA Galaxy (5)
Top Goalscorer: Chris Wondolowski -
149, and counting
A big moment: In 2020, Inter Miami –
a team owned by David Beckham –
will enter the league pyramid.

10 THE PREMIER LEAGUE

Location: England and Wales
Founded: 1992 (although the top flight of
English football has been going since 1888)
Most Titles: Manchester United (20)
Top Goalscorer of all time: Jimmy
Greaves - 357
**Top Goalscorer since Premier League
formation:** Alan Shearer - 260 goals
A big moment: The relegation favourites,
Leicester City won the title in 2016.

11 A-LEAGUE

Location: Australia
Founded: 2004 (previously National Soccer
League from 1974)
Most Titles: Melbourne Victory and Perth
Glory (4)
Top Goalscorer: Besart Berisha - 116
A big moment: In 2018, Central Coast
Mariners offered 100m world record holder
Usain Bolt a professional contract.

AMAZING STADIUMS

There is hardly anything that feels as exciting as approaching a stadium on match day. The smells, and the colours, and the sounds, and the prospect of watching your team lose 4-0: unbeatable. Stadiums are big, imposing places where dreams can be made or broken. Some of them stand out more than others. Here you will discover some of the most iconic football stadiums the world has to offer.

CAMP NOU

Barcelona's Camp Nou has the largest capacity of any football stadium in Europe. It can hold 99,354 spectators.

The seats one of the stands spell out the phrase 'MORE THAN A CLUB' in Catalan, which is the club motto. Camp Nou has hosted many famous games, but not all of them have involved the Barcelona team. Camp Nou hosted the final five games of the 1982 World Cup and the Olympic football final in 1992, as well as the European Cup/Champions League final in 1989 and 1999.

In the 1989 European Cup final, Milan manager Arrigo Sacchi played some of the best Italian players of the time: Galli, Tassotti, Costacurta, Baresi, Maldini, Donadoni, Ancelotti and Colombo alongisde Dutch players Rijkaard, Gullit and Van Basten.

The 1999 Champions League final was Manchester United's famous comeback against Bayern Munich. United were 1-0 down until Teddy Sherringham and Ole Gunnar Solskjaer scored to win the cup and complete United's treble of 1999, made up of the Premier League, FA Cup and Champions League titles.

LA BOMBONERA

La Bombonera is the home of Boca Juniors in Argentina. In Spanish, La Bombonera means 'the chocolate box'. The stadium is called this because the shape of the building reminded the club president of a box of chocolates.

La Bombonera was built in 1940 and holds 49,000 people. The stadium has amazing acoustics (the way in which sound projects and travels around a building). The supporters are called *la doce*, which means 'the twelfth man', because they are so supportive, they are as helpful as having a twelfth player.

Don't be fooled by the sweet name, the Chocolate Box is renowned as one of the most intimidating football stadiums to play at in the world.

STADE VÉLODROME

This stadium has a very distinctive domed roof and is home to the Olympique de Marseille team in France. The Vélodrome can hold 67,394 people and if all the rows of seats were put side by side, they would measure over 32 miles.

The Vélodrome hosted two games at the 1938 World Cup, six games at Euro 2016, and seven at the 1998 World Cup, including the quarter final between the Netherlands and Argentina in which Dennis Bergkamp scored one of his greatest goals ever.

In the last five minutes of the Netherlands – Argentina game, the score was 1-1. With two minutes to go, Dutch player Frank de Boer launched the ball to Dennis Bergkamp, who kicked it between two Argentinian defenders, smashing it into the top corner of the goal and winning the game for the Netherlands.

WEMBLEY

Wembley Stadium is one of the most famous football stadiums in the world. Since its reopening in 2007, it can hold 90,000 fans and is home to England's national football team.

Wembley was briefly the home of Tottenham Hotspur, while their new stadium at White Hart Lane was under construction between 2017 and 2019.

Wembley Stadium hosts the FA Cup final every year. It has also hosted seven Champions League finals. For England the most important game played here was the 1966 World Cup final. England beat West Germany 4-2. Geoff Hurst scored a hat-trick and Bobby Moore lifted the iconic Jules Rimet trophy.

MELBOURNE CRICKET GROUND

The Melbourne Cricket Ground is the tenth-largest stadium in the world. Built all the way back in 1853 and with a capacity of 100,024, it's a big, big old stadium and the largest in the Southern Hemisphere.

It hosts Aussie Rules Football in the winter and cricket in the summer. The first football match hosted there was between Victoria and Tasmania in 1912 and it hosted the Olympic Games in 1956.

Lots of teams play at the MCG when they tour during the off-season. When Manchester City took on Real Madrid in the International Champions Cup in 2014, 99,382 fans went to watch.

WESTFALENSTADION

Westfalenstadion is home to Borussia Dortmund. The stadium is also known as Signal Iduna Park and can hold 81,365 fans.

The Südtribüne is the name for the standing area of the stadium. It is the biggest standing area in any European stadium and can hold 24,454 people. It is nicknamed The Yellow Wall because when the fans hold their yellow scarves and flags it looks like a big wall of yellow.

One of the stands at Tottenham Hotspur's new White Hart Lane stadium is modelled on Westfalenstadion's *Südtribüne*.

In 2006, Germany played Italy at Westfalenstadion in the World Cup semi-finals. The score was 0-0 after 90 minutes and it went to extra time. It looked as though the match would go to penalties, but Fabio Grosso and Alessandro Del Piero scored in the 119th and 120th minutes to put Italy into the World Cup final and make the German fans cry.

SAN SIRO

Also known as the Giuseppe Meazza Stadium, San Siro is home to both A.C. Milan and Internazionale, nicknamed 'Inter'. It holds 80,018 spectators and is one of the oldest and most famous grounds.

San Siro hosted six of the 1990 World Cup games, as well as Champions League finals in 1965, 1970, 2001 and 2016. Three of the games at the 1934 World Cup were also played at San Siro.

In 2003, A.C. Milan had to play Inter in the Champions League semi-finals, which are played over two games. If the score is tied at the end of those games, whichever team scored the most goals away from home go through. However, A.C. Milan and Inter were both playing at home in both legs! The first ended 0-0, and the second ended 1-1. You would think that this result meant a draw. But, before the games took place, it had been decided that the first leg would count as A.C. Milan's home game, and the second leg would count as Inter's home game. This meant that A.C. Milan went through on away goals, despite both teams playing at home for both legs. How confusing!

SOCCER CITY

South Africa held the continent's first ever World Cup in 2010, a tournament that screamed with the sound of the Vuvuzela, a plastic horn that everyone in the crowd seemed to have.

The final was held here, in Johannesburg, in the brilliantly named Soccer City. Imagine a city just for football! It's also known as the First National Bank Stadium, which isn't as fun, or The Calabash, which is the name of a traditional African pot that it resembles. During the league, it's the home for Kaizer Chiefs FC who play in the South African Premier Soccer League.

The stadium was where Nelson Mandela, an incredibly important man who fought for equality between races in South Africa, gave a speech when he was released from jail. It's an important place, and the World Cup final saw over 84,000 people watch Iker Casillas lift the cup.

THE ROSE BOWL

In the summer of 1994, the World Cup was held in the United States of America for the first time. The final of the tournament, Brazil v Italy, was played at The Rose Bowl, a huge roofless stadium in Pasadena, a suburb of Los Angeles in California. The stadium holds 92,542 people, and was completely packed out for the final.

The game itself, played after four weeks of games in the heat, was a slow-burner and was 0-0 after both 90 minutes and extra time: the first and last World Cup final to have no goals throughout. It went to penalties, which Brazil won 3-2, with Roberto Baggio – nicknamed *Il Divin Codino*, meaning The Divine Ponytail, because of his hair – missing the decisive penalty. Baggio was distraught, the Brazilians were ecstatic and the Rose Bowl had seen one of the strangest World Cup finals of all time.

KITS HALL OF FAME

Is there any better feeling than putting on your favourite football kit?
On a practical level, football shirts are there to help players identify who is on their team, so they can pass the ball to them. But to fans and to players, they mean much, much more. They're not just for wearing on the pitch, they're for wearing when you're with your friends, or having dinner, or practising in the garden. Football kits are sometimes amazing, sometimes silly and sometimes rubbish... These are our pick of the bunch. What do you think?

PLYMOUTH ARGYLE (UK), 1965

The beautiful green-and-black horizontal stripes of this strip contrast perfectly with the fresh white of the jersey. The big crest with the billowing sails of the *Mayflower* ship adds real drama right in the middle of the shirt.

USSR, 1966

The USSR's (now Russia) 1966 kit was a plain, red sweatshirt with 'CCCP' written across the front. In Russia they use a different alphabet, and this spelled USSR. The design was simple but a classic.

MARSEILLE (FRANCE), HOME, 1971

This strip has plain, white shorts and a smart crew neck collar featuring the colours of the French flag. The word 'BUT', which means 'GOAL' in French is bravely smacked across the front of it in capital letters.

NETHERLANDS, HOME, 1972
SPECIFICALLY JOHAN CRUYFF'S

Puma and adidas were founded by rival brothers. Cruyff was sponsored by Puma, but the shirt was made by adidas. To stay loyal to Puma, Cruyff ripped the third stripe off the arm of his adidas shirt, and managed to make it look cooler in the process.

This strip was designed by Ralph Lauren and has a striking logo. The large numbers are bold and stylish. It was worn by Carlos Alberto and Franz Beckenbauer, which helps add to its iconic status.

BOCA JUNIORS (ARGENTINA), HOME, 1981

If you see a blue shirt with a big horizontal yellow stripe across the middle, it can only be one team: Boca Juniors. The shirt is classic, simple and timeless.

LAZIO (ITALY), HOME, 1982

This shirt has an eagle with its wings spread, in the team colours, right over the front. Very nice, Lazio, *bravissimo!*

JUVENTUS (ITALY), HOME, 1983

Michel Platini, Marco Tardelli and Cesare Prandelli wore this classic black-and-white striped number with a massive white collar. They looked fantastic in it.

DENMARK, HOME, 1986

A harlequin-style shirt split into quarters, and two of those quarters have super-thin red-and-white stripes in them. The players who wore it became style itself.

HOLLAND, HOME, 1986

With adidas stripes down the sleeves, a cool pattern that makes it look like a reflector for your bike and traditional orange with chunky black numbering, this shirt belongs in the hall of fame.

MANCHESTER CITY (UK), AWAY, 1988

A gorgeous shirt covered in burgundy-and-white stripes, with a traditional sky-blue collar and the sponsor 'brother' emblazoned on the chest.

WEST GERMANY, HOME, 1988

This black-and-white shirt is such a classic that it was remade in 2018, and it looked just as good second time around.

GRÊMIO (BRAZIL), HOME, 1990

You just don't see thick black-and-sky-blue stripes separated by narrower white stripes enough on football kits these days.

ENGLAND, HOME, 1990

With Umbro tape around the sleeves and a crisp collar, this shirt is so smart you could almost get away with wearing it to a wedding.

SAMPDORIA (ITALY), HOME, 1991

This shirt's colours, design and badge come together in perfect harmony to make a very stylish piece.

MARSEILLE (FRANCE), HOME, 1992

The three light blue stripes coming over the shoulder are like a pat on the back from a giant three-toed bear. It's no wonder they won the Champions League.

AUSTRALIA, HOME, 1993

This is a legendary piece of sports clothing. The media called it 'the pizza vomit shirt' and, well, they were probably right. The Aussies wore it for their unsuccessful qualifying campaign for the 1994 World Cup, and it's possible that nobody has worn it since.

NAGOYA GRAMPUS EIGHT (JAPAN), HOME, 1994

Arsène Wenger's team wore these red jerseys with diagonal yellow-and-white stripes in 1994. They each had their own name plastered over the chest, where a sponsor's name would usually be.

USA, AWAY, 1994

The stars stretched over the shirt make it look like the US flag billowing in the wind. It shall remain hoisted at full mast in this book for evermore.

ESTONIA, GOALKEEPER, HOME, 1997

Like your grandma's favourite curtains that she flatly refuses to get rid of, but somehow good.

MEXICO, HOME, 1998

This design combines Aztec patterns and the giant face of the Aztec god of death in various shades of green. A masterpiece.

FRANCE, AWAY, 2013

This is very similar to the classic '70s Marseille kit but with a polo shirt-style collar and a classy duck-egg blue colour.

MADUREIRA SPORTING CLUB (CUBA), GOALKEEPER, HOME, 2013

The whole shirt was a Cuban flag with a big picture of Cuban leader Che Guevara on it. You either love this one or you hate it.

NIGERIA, HOME, 2018

This shirt features 1990s-style zig-zag stripes. It is green and white on the body and black and white on the sleeves. It was easily the best kit at World Cup 2018.

JAPAN WOMEN'S, HOME, 2019

The 2019 World Cup was the first where women had kits designed specifically for... women. It is ridiculous that it took so long for this to happen. There were some great shirts in this World Cup, but this was probably the best.

HOW TO...

Now you know the history of the game, let's learn how to play it like a pro. You don't have to be the best player in the world to enjoy it – football is about running around on a piece of grass with your friends, but it's also fun to get better at it. And coach Chris is going to help you get up to scratch.

HOW TO TAKE THE PERFECT SHOT
LIKE JI SO-YUN

Being able to finish, or take a good shot, is crucial in football. It's how you're going to score most of your goals. And Ji So-yun is very good at scoring goals. When she is bearing-down on a goal, she is usually going at full speed, causing havoc in the opposition defence, limbs moving all over the place to distract the defenders. But in her head, all is calm.

If you see an opportunity to shoot, start thinking about the ball and the ball only. It's just you and the ball. The goal will stay exactly where it is.

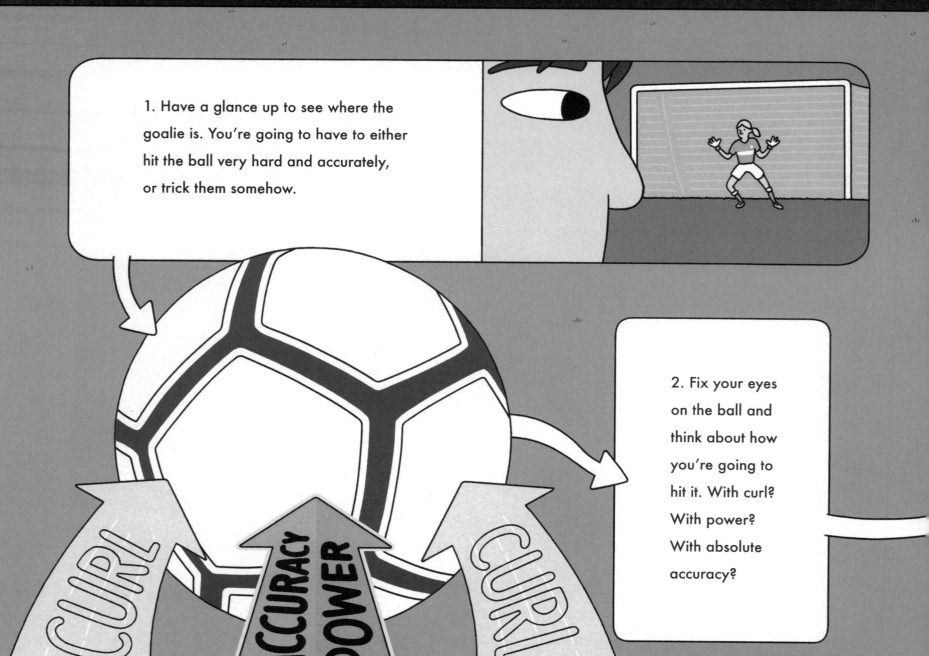

1. Have a glance up to see where the goalie is. You're going to have to either hit the ball very hard and accurately, or trick them somehow.

2. Fix your eyes on the ball and think about how you're going to hit it. With curl? With power? With absolute accuracy?

CURL   ACCURACY   POWER   CURL

GOAL!

JI SO-YUN

Born in 1991, Ji So-yun grew up in Seoul in South Korea. She started her career playing at INAC Kobe Leonessa. She moved to Chelsea in 2013, and is now considered one of the best players in the world. Ji is the youngest ever goalscorer for South Korea. She was only 15 years and 282 days old when she scored her first international goal, and is now South Korea's all-time top scorer. Ji also scored the only goal in the first FA Women's Cup Final to be held at Wembley Stadium in 2015.

4. Don't stop your foot when you get to the ball. Follow through with your laces, your leg and your whole body.

3. Place your standing leg close to the ball and strike right through it, making sure you follow through to get the most power.

All good strikers know exactly where the goal is, no matter where they are on the pitch. The goal doesn't move, so always keep it in mind.

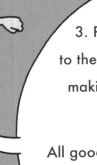

Bonus tip: Try asking your goalkeeper friends what type of shots they find most difficult to save, then practise those shots until you can do them with your eyes closed.

HOW TO MAKE THE PERFECT SLIDE TACKLE
LIKE ALESSANDRO NESTA

To do a wicked slide tackle, you have to be certain of what is going to happen in two or three seconds' time, otherwise you'll commit a foul or hurt your opponent. Try and work out where the players around you are heading and where they will be. Alessandro Nesta was good at slide tackling because he watched and played so much football that he always knew what his opponent was going to do. And, by learning so much from watching, he could commit himself to a heroic, beautiful sliding tackle.

1. Analyse where the ball is now, and how fast the opposition player who has the ball is running. Which way are they likely to run and how quickly? When are you most likely going to be able to nick the ball? Anticipation is key.

2. Start your manoeuvre. Run at the right pace for where you expect the ball to be when you're going to make your tackle. Head towards that spot and get ready to make your slide.

LONGEST SLIDE TACKLE EVER

Born in 1974 in Plaistow, East London, Sol Campbell was the youngest of 12 children. He was an amazing footballer as a child and trained at England's prestigious schoolboy training camp Lilleshall. Sol won lots of trophies, mostly for Arsenal. A slide tackle he made in the 24th minute of a game while playing for England against Croatia is considered the longest slide tackle ever. Many people say he's still sliding now, but they are exaggerating.

3. Once you're close, start to think about putting all of your weight towards the ground so that you can slide smoothly towards the ball.

5. Get up, move away from the opposition and hold on to possession.

4. Slide on your thigh, with your other leg stretched towards the ball. Move all of your weight towards that foot and slide straight through the ball, aiming to hook it towards your body to keep possession.

ALESSANDRO NESTA

Nesta is one of the greatest defenders of all time, having won the Serie A award for Defender of the Year four times. When Nesta was playing, Serie A was known for its impeccable defenders, so to be named the best in Italy four times is quite an honour. Nesta also won Serie A three times, the Champions League twice with A.C. Milan, and the World Cup with Italy in 2006.

One of the secrets to Nesta's success was that he put the ball first. When he tackled his opponent, he always made sure the ball stuck with him or moved away from danger. The perfect slide tackle should be clean, safe and perfectly timed. So get out your crystal ball and your tea leaves and start predicting the future like Alessandro Nesta.

HOW TO TAKE THE PERFECT SET PIECE
LIKE DAVID BECKHAM

David Beckham was the king of curve. He had all the makings of a superstar with his boy band looks and immaculate passing, crossing and shooting techniques. Beckham was a very talented young player but he spent long hours training on his own in the local park in order to perfect his signature moves. He was notorious for putting curve on the ball, which made his set pieces difficult to defend against. His free kicks and corners would curve and swerve so impressively they seemed to defy physics.

1. Place the ball in a tuft of grass that allows your foot to connect cleanly. Make sure the ball doesn't sit too high on the long grass or the ball will loop too high when kicked. Also, don't squash the ball too deep into the tuft or it will be hard to get enough lift.

2. Have a look at where your teammates are, or if you're practising on your own, have a think about where they would be. You want to curve the ball so it reaches them at just the right moment.

3. Now focus on the ball. Think about which part of it you want to hit with your foot. Striking it to the left or right of the middle means it will spin in the air and curl, making it difficult for defenders to follow it. You want a nice, big arc.

Sounds difficult, but once you start to hit it sweetly, you won't want to stop. You'll be curving the ball all day. You can practise by finding a bucket, setting it up at different heights and trying to kick the ball into the bucket without the ball bouncing.

5. Make sure you follow through with your foot after you connect with the ball. You want to get enough pace on the ball for it to confuse defenders and reach your teammate, who can tap it into the net.

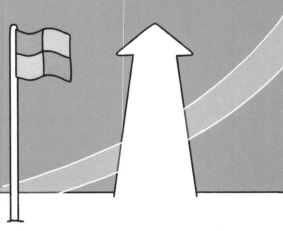

4. Start your run towards the ball and place your non-kicking foot close to it, then move your foot through the ball, connecting with the bit that is between the top of your foot and the side. Keep practising until you start to perfect this skill.

DAVID BECKHAM

Becks is one of the most famous footballers of the past 30 years, and for good reason. He was the first English player to win the top league in four different countries: England (Manchester United), Spain (Real Madrid), Italy (A.C. Milan) and the USA (LA Galaxy).

He was a set piece specialist, and once scored from the halfway line on the opening day of the Premier League season in 1996.

In 1998 he almost ruined his reputation. He was fouled when playing against Argentina in a World Cup match. He was so frustrated that he kicked Diego Simeone (later the famous manager of Atlético Madrid), who stumbled to the ground. Beckham was sent off for his behaviour. England lost 4-3 on penalties and were knocked out of the World Cup.

The newspapers said nasty things about young David, but he reacted in the right way. Instead of getting angry or hiding from his mistakes, he practised and trained as hard as he could, and made himself into one of the best midfielders in the world, eventually being signed by Real Madrid and regaining the respect of football fans across the world.

HOW TO PLAY THE PERFECT LONG BALL
LIKE XABI ALONSO

Liverpool fans used to sing, 'He is the midfield maestro, and his passes are so delightful, everybody wants to know, Al-on-so, Al-on-so, Al-on-so' and he is the long-ball hero. The long ball or long pass is very important because it means you can reach a teammate of yours on the other side of the pitch while taking the opposition players out of the game.

1. The first thing you should do whenever you get the ball is look up from the ball and around yourself. When you're planning to play a long ball, take a look at who has space around them for you to send it to.

2. Decide who you are passing to. Move the ball to your stronger foot and think about whether you want the ball to go straight to your teammate's feet or a little further ahead of them so they can run onto it.

XABI ALONSO

Born in 1981, Xabi Alonso was a very clever central midfielder who played for Real Sociedad, Liverpool, Real Madrid and Bayern Munich. He has won the World Cup, the European Championships, the Champions League, the FA Cup, La Liga, the Copa del Rey (Spanish Cup), the Bundesliga and the DFB-Pokal (German Cup). He once scored from his own half for Liverpool against Newcastle United... a long ball straight into the goal. It was beautiful and unbelievable.

4. Strike through the ball with the laces on your boot and start to move straightaway. Don't spend too long soaking up the glory from your amazing long ball. Your next job is to be in space to help your teammate out.

When played well, the long ball can defeat a high press and be an effective counter-attacking technique. It can take multiple opponents out of the game in a short amount of time. They look great and kicking a ball far feels great.

3. Who have you got to get it past, and how? Think about the height and weight of your kick. Do you want to hit it as hard as possible to get it over the opposition, or loop it up into the air slightly so that your teammate can take out one of the opposing players when they receive it?

HOW TO TAKE PENALTIES
LIKE MATT LE TISSIER

Penalties don't have an awful lot to do with technique. If you can kick a ball, you can take a penalty. The thing about penalties is that are all in your head. They're all about mastering your nerves, making decisions and having confidence in yourself when under pressure.

GOAL!

1. Think positive thoughts. Goalkeepers are like dogs and can smell fear and nerves. If you show fear, you will miss, so thinking positively is the most important thing.

3. Be adaptable. As you are about to kick, see if the goalie commits early to one side or the other. If you react quickly, you can roll the ball into the opposite corner to score an easy goal.

2. Pick a part of the goal to aim

MATT LE TISSIER

Matt Le Tissier was Southampton's star player of the 1990s. He regularly scored effortless wonder-goals. He took 49 penalties in his career and only missed one of them.

That's a phenomenal record and even better than Lionel Messi and Cristiano Ronaldo. He was a bold decision maker and this helped him put the ball in the back of the net time after time.

Bonus tip: Practise a lot and always put yourself forward to take a penalty in a game. It's a totally different feeling taking penalties in front of a crowd rather than in your back garden.

HOW TO DO NUTMEGS
LIKE LUIS SUÁREZ

To nutmeg somebody means to play the ball between their legs in order to get past them. Some people think that this term comes from cockney rhyming slang, in which legs are called nutmegs. The ball goes through your legs, or through your nutmegs. It's something that makes you feel a bit confused and then embarrassed if it happens to you, but if you do it, you feel pretty smart, and it is really useful. There are a few different ways of doing it.

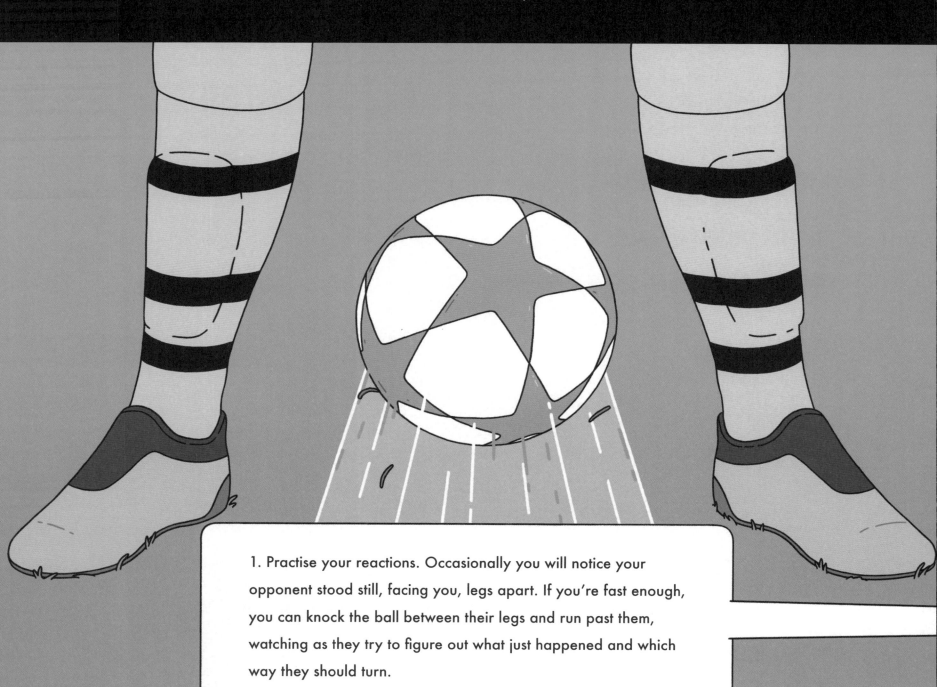

1. Practise your reactions. Occasionally you will notice your opponent stood still, facing you, legs apart. If you're fast enough, you can knock the ball between their legs and run past them, watching as they try to figure out what just happened and which way they should turn.

3. Don't kick the ball too far through the opponent's legs. Remember that unless you are playing a pass through their legs, you will have to run around them and meet the ball at the other side.

2. Create a chance to nutmeg an opponent by feigning to run in a certain direction, and as the opponent moves to chase you, knock the ball between their now open legs. Then sprint away, leaving the defender considering whether or not to just get their legs sewn together and hop instead of walking for the rest of their life.

LUIS SUÁREZ

Luis Suárez is really good at making a fool of himself, but he's much better at making fools out of opposition players. He has been banned for biting opponent players on three occasions in his career, and once stopped a goal from going in with his hand when Uruguay were playing Ghana in the World Cup quarter finals. He was sent off, but Ghana missed the subsequent penalty and ended up losing the game. Suárez, however, is an unbelievably good striker and an expert at nutmegging defenders.

Bonus tip: Give them the eyes. You know, freak them out. Look in one direction as though you're travelling that way, then head in the opposite direction. They'll move one leg, then you can pop the ball through the space between their legs.

LIKE DENNIS BERGKAMP

Your first touch is the way in which you adapt your body to control the ball when you receive it. You need to receive it in a way that makes your next step on the pitch easy. You might cushion it with your thigh, trap it under the sole of your foot, or take it in your stride while you run. The players with the best first touch make it look like they were born with a football next to them. Like Maradona, who even at the age of 10 used to be paid to do kick-ups in the centre circle at professional club Argentinos Juniors. Oh, Diego!

1. Look around you before, or as the pass is on its way to you. Know where every player is on the pitch, especially the players closest to you, and decide whether you are going to shoot, pass or dribble once you've controlled the ball.

2. Now you know where the other players are and what you're going to do with the ball, do not take your eye off it until you have controlled it.

4. Don't focus on just trapping the ball. Trapping the ball dead is sometimes useful but often it just slows you down and means you have to waste time taking another touch to get the ball to where you need it to be. The longer you take to control the ball, the longer the opposition have to organise themselves and defend your attack.

3. Judge the flight of the ball. Take notice of how quickly the ball is moving, whether it is spinning and whether the ball is on the floor or coming down from a height. These things will affect how you cushion the ball. If the ball is arriving fast and hard, try using the inside of your foot, allowing your foot to move backwards with the ball slightly to bring the ball to a stop. If you just hold your foot in a fixed position, the ball will bounce off you and you will lose it.

DENNIS BERGKAMP

Dennis Bergkamp was a Dutch forward for Ajax, Inter and Arsenal. Have you ever played that game where you and a friend have to throw an egg to each other from further and further away, and you have to be really careful not to break the egg when you catch it? That's how Dennis Bergkamp treated a football. He did not panic or use force when the ball came to him, he welcomed the ball. He cared for the ball. He probably tucked a football into bed at night and told it bedtime stories and sang lullabies to it. Footballs were obviously grateful for this tender, loving care, and tended to do whatever Bergkamp wanted them to do, which had something to do with them ending up in the back of the net in the next five seconds or so.

HOW TO PLAY THE PERFECT THROUGH BALL
LIKE XAVI

A 'through ball' is a pass that is played forwards, ahead of your teammate, so that they can run onto the ball. A through ball is usually played through a defensive line and is a great way to penetrate a stubborn defence, especially if the opposition is holding a high defensive line.

XAVI

Xavi Hernández was probably the best central midfielder of the 2000s and early 2010s. Xavi and Andrés Iniesta ran Barcelona and Spain's midfield in their most successful eras. It seemed as though they could read each other's minds and they made lots of short passes while moving around the pitch at speed. Xavi's spatial awareness and ability to keep the opposition players at a distance was miraculous. Xavi achieved this by constantly picturing the game three or four seconds in the future.

1. Try to predict where the opposition defenders are going to move to next, where your teammates are going to run to and where space is going to appear.

2. Pass the ball. Control the pace and weight of the kick, so that your teammate can control, pass or shoot with minimal effort. It is useful to kick the ball at the bottom or side to make it spin in the air and curve away from a defender and towards your teammate.

3. Make sure there is space behind the defence for your teammate to run into.

HOW TO BEAT THE OFFSIDE TRAP
LIKE FERNANDO TORRES

An offside trap is a defensive strategy in which the defenders form a straight line across the pitch and attempt to move forward at the same time in order to catch attackers offside when the ball is played to them. It's an effective tactic but a risky one and can leave a team vulnerable if a striker is an expert in beating the offside trap, like Fernando Torres.

1. Be fast.

2. Communicate with your teammates. Tell them when you want the ball to be played. Show them with your arms and with your voice. Discuss what sort of passes you like to receive before the match.

3. Time your run to perfection. The best way to do this is to position yourself a few metres back from the defensive line. Just as your teammate is about to pass to you, start sprinting at the defensive line, so that you are at full speed at the moment when they start running. This will allow you to reach the ball before the defenders without being caught offside.

FERNANDO TORRES

Beating the offside trap was Torres' special skill. He did this especially well in the 2012 Champions League semi final for Chelsea against Barcelona. You cannot be offside if you are in your own half. When Barcelona pushed up to try and score a late goal, Torres waited near the halfway line, in his own half and when the ball was cleared towards him, he was able to sprint towards the goal without having to pass any defenders. The goal put Chelsea into the final, prompting commentator Gary Neville to make one of the strangest happy noises ever made by a human being, live on telly.

HOW TO DO THE PERFECT ATTACKING HEADER
LIKE DIDIER DROGBA

An attacking header is a way of scoring a goal with your head. Your noggin. Your bean. More specifically your forehead. You use your forehead because it's the strongest part of your skull. Sometimes, you might want to use an attacking header as a pass to one of your teammates, but mostly you use this move when trying to score a goal.

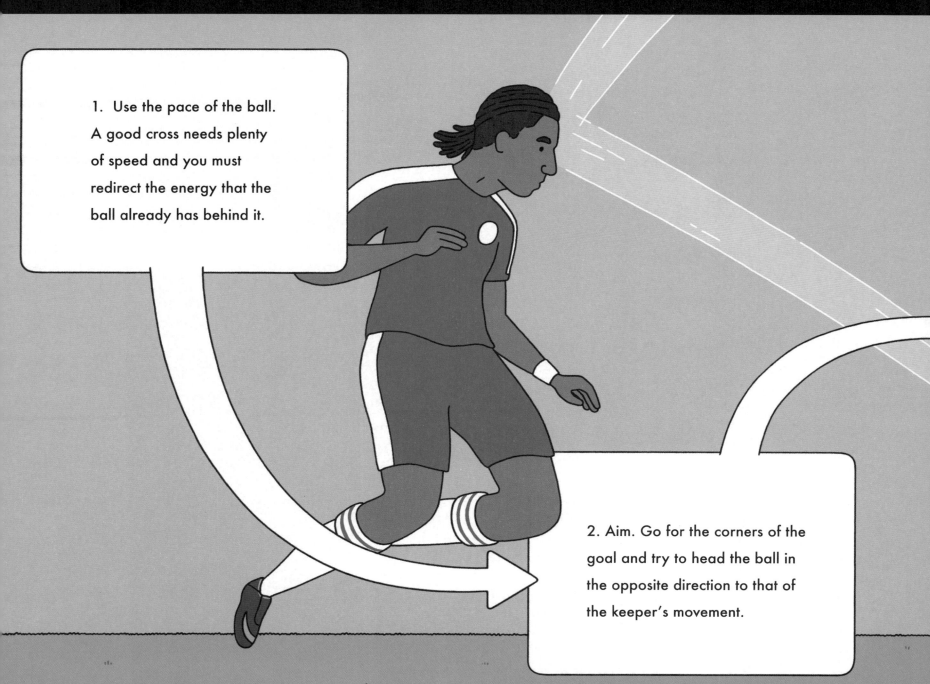

1. Use the pace of the ball. A good cross needs plenty of speed and you must redirect the energy that the ball already has behind it.

2. Aim. Go for the corners of the goal and try to head the ball in the opposite direction to that of the keeper's movement.

4. Keep your eyes open. Watch the ball until your head makes contact with it, otherwise you might accidentally miss your forehead and hit a different part of your head, giving you less control.

3. Head the ball downwards with your forehead. Drogba would often attempt to head the ball downwards, towards the goal and into the ground. It is more difficult to judge the flight of the ball if it is headed downwards. It also means the keeper has to quickly get down to the ground in time to save it.

DIDIER DROGBA

Didier Drogba was born in Abidjan in the Ivory Coast, but as a child he moved away to live with his uncle on the outskirts of Paris. In 679 games for Le Mans, Marseille and Chelsea he scored 297 goals, as well as 65 goals in 105 games for his national Ivory Coast team. He won the African Footballer of the Year in 2006 and 2009, and even had a hand in halting a civil war in his home country. Amongst all of this, Didier was fantastic at heading the ball.

Bonus tip: If you head the ball towards the side of the goal where a cross has been hit from, you're most likely to trick the keeper into going the wrong way.

HOW TO DO THE PERFECT DEFENSIVE HEADER
LIKE KALIDOU KOULIBALY

A defensive header is a way of stopping and clearing an opposition team's attack with your head. It's used most often if the opposition has played a long ball – a big, aerial kick from goalkeepers or defenders that is aimed towards the strikers – or a cross from the wings. To slow down the attack, or stop it completely if at all possible, you want to get as much distance and air on the ball as possible... and if the attack is looking super dangerous, just head the ball out for a throw-in or corner. Get rid of it!

1. Jump! You don't have to be tall. What you lack in height you can make up for by jumping.

2. Be strong and don't allow attackers to muscle you off the ball. You must be able to stand your ground. You don't have to be big, but you have to be steadfast.

3. Practise your timing. If you jump too quickly or too late to meet the ball, the move will be doomed.

6. Get in position. Aim to give yourself space to have a little run-up for your jump. Performing a header after a run-up is most effective. It gives you more momentum than jumping from standing still.

5. Always use your forehead and make sure you attack the ball instead of letting the ball hit you. If you don't, it might hurt.

4. Get the ball to safety. If you can safely head the ball to a teammate, fantastic. If you can't, focus instead on distance and height, to give your team a chance to regroup and reorganise.

KALIDOU KOULIBALY

Born in France in 1991 to Senegalese parents, Kalidou Koulibaly moved from Metz in France, to Genk in Belgium, to Napoli in Italy, where his talents truly flourished. Under manager Maurizio Sarri, Kalidou became one of the greatest defenders in the world. His positioning, reading of the game, tackling and heading are incredible. You'd do very well to get past Kalidou Koulibaly.

Bonus tip: Scream or shout your name, or your nickname, as loud as you can when attacking the ball. It makes you sound scary, and might distract the opposition player.

WEIRD AND WONDERFUL

The aim of the game is to get the ball into a goal and to stop your opponent from scoring. What could be more straightforward? But football is very strange. From the way we describe things that happen in the game (a fox in the box) to the way we celebrate a goal (by pretending to be a robot) or do our hair (shaving it all off except for a triangle at the front)... deep down, we all know that the reason we love football is because it is a strange old game.

THE HAIRCUTS

When you have to wear exactly the same kits as your teammates, hair is one of the few ways you can show the world your individuality. Here are some of the strangest and best haircuts in the game.

DAVID BECKHAM'S MOHAWK

Becks is famous for his trend-setting, varied hairstyles over the years, but the mohawk is probably the most iconic. Soon after he debuted his new chop, kids all over the world started to request the 'Beckham Mohawk'.

TARIBO WEST'S GREEN BUNCHES

Taribo West was a hero of the 1996 Olympics and part of the famous Nigeria side who won the tournament — the first African nation ever to do so. Taribo's signature look was to have no hair except for two green bunches tied tight on top of his head. It's a very bold look.

AJARA NCHOUT'S STYLE

Cameroonian forward Ajara Nchout has played all over the world, from Sweden to Russia to the States to Norway, scoring tons of goals along the way. All the while, she never fails to have amazing hair.

PAUL POGBA'S ARTISTRY

Paul Pogba's hair is art. He has had all sorts of shaved and dyed looks. Most famously he had leopard print and red-and-orange flames on the sides of his head.

CARLOS VALDERRAMA'S BLONDE 'FRO

Valderrama was instantly recognisable on the pitch. The Colombian number 10 sported a giant, blonde, afro-style haircut topped off with a big, equally magnificent moustache. Carlos Valderrama: great at football, terrible at hide and seek.

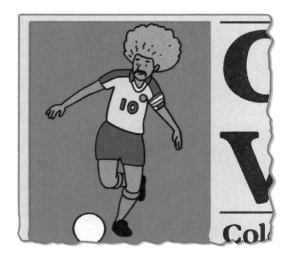

CHRIS WADDLE'S MULLET

It may be strange to think that in the 1980s, the mullet was fashionable, but it was and Waddle had a magnificent one. Waddle worshipped the mullet. He was best mates with the mullet and he couldn't let it go.

THE ENTIRE ROMANIA WORLD CUP SQUAD OF 1998

Romania had a team meeting just before the start of World Cup '98 in France. At this team meeting, the coach told his players that if they qualified for the knock-out rounds after two games, he would shave his head. The players told him that if he did that, then in return they would all dye their hair blonde. It happened, and they all looked great.

RONALDO'S NOTHING BUT FRINGE

This is probably the strangest thing that has ever been on a person's head, but if you're the best striker in the world, you can do whatever you like and people will still think it's cool. At the 2002 World Cup, Ronaldo de Lima turned up for Brazil with a completely shaved head, except for a triangle of hair at the front of his head that sort of looked like a third of a pizza.

MICHELLE AKERS

Look, Michelle Akers is one of the most fantastic footballers ever to grace the sport. She won the FIFA Player of the Century award. Maybe her power came from her magnificent, voluminous hair.

DAVID SEAMAN'S PONYTAIL

David Seaman was Arsenal's legendary goalkeeper during the 1990s and 2000s. He was an outstanding goalkeeper but, unfortunately, he is remembered for two things. Firstly, for when Ronaldinho chipped him from about 35 metres away with a free kick in the England v Brazil match at World Cup 2002. Secondly, for suddenly deciding that it would be a superb idea to grow a big shiny ponytail.

OLIVIER GIROUD

There is nothing funny about French forward Olivier Giroud's hair, and that's exactly why he is here. His hair is perfect. We don't know how he does it.

THE CELEBRATIONS

The history of the game, the evolution of the ball and the changes in formation are all very important things to know about. But the best moment is when someone scores a goal. It is the best feeling in the world, and people celebrate in some bizarre ways. Here are some that were famous for specific players, and some that people all over the world do every day.

THE ONE HAND RAISED

This is a classic and was most famously employed by Alan Shearer, who was a brilliant striker. This celebration is simple, effective and satisfying. It's a salute to the fans to let them know you love them.

THE KNEE SLIDE

Imagine that you're playing for your childhood club in your home debut. The fans are cheering you on. There are scarves with the team colours on everywhere. You pick up the ball just outside the box and curl in a worldie. What does your brain tell you? 'Knee slide. Do a big knee slide right over to the corner flag. That will be absolutely great!' So you do.

ROCKING THE BABY

This is quite a rare celebration that tends to be used by players who have just had a baby. Rocking The Baby was first used by Brazilian forward Bebeto, following the birth of his son during the 1994 World Cup in the USA. When you score a goal, how do you feel? Well, usually you feel very happy. Bebeto was obviously overjoyed to have a new baby boy, and so when he scored, he did what came naturally and thought of his son.

JUMPING INTO THE CROWD

This celebration does not come recommended as you will almost certainly be shown a yellow card by the referee. However, in the past, people have felt the moment take them and you jump in and start hugging everyone around you while they chant your name. Sometimes you just have to go and hug the people who love you.

THE AEROPLANE

When you score a goal, sometimes it can feel as though you are flying and circling around the pitch looking down at all the unfortunate people who haven't scored a goal. Steve Bull did this particular move 306 times for Wolves.

THE STAND STILL WITH YOUR ARMS OUT

This is only to be used following absolutely jaw-dropping goals, otherwise you'll just look a bit silly. It says, 'Look at me and feast your eyes upon the glorious footballer you see before you.' Stand still and soak up the glory that is rightfully being showered upon you.

THE NO TIME TO WASTE

A move that is perfect for when time is running out. Imagine that your team is 3-1 down with five minutes to go. You score a goal but you only have five minutes left to get the draw or the win. You want to get the ball back in play again as soon as possible so you collect the ball and run it straight back to the centre circle so the match can start again. There is no time for big celebrations here. After all, you're a team player and it's not all about you.

KISSING THE GRASS

You often hear people talking about the 'hallowed turf' of a stadium, meaning that it is so special it is almost sacred. Kissing the grass is a show of respect to the place you love.

JUMPING ON THE MANAGER

Some players have bad relationships with their managers and some players idolise them. If your coach has helped you with your technique and helped you through hard times, then the first thing you're going to want to do when you score is run over to them, jump on them and give them a big, squeezy hug. Never forget that managers need hugs too.

THE MILLA DANCE

Roger Milla from the Cameroon national team was the oldest ever World Cup goalscorer in 1990. He celebrated by dancing around the corner flag like a funky chicken.

THE RAPINOE POWER STATUE

Megan Rapinoe from the USA scores goals, and she scores them often. As an advocate for equality Rapinoe said that she would not attend the White House to meet the President if the US won the World Cup because he is not an advocate for equality. President Trump responded and told her not to disrespect the country. The following game, Megan scored, stood still, raised her hands to the sky, grinned and stood in an epic pose like a Greek statue. She stood in defiance of the President and stood for what she believed in. Many people recognised this as a wonderful power pose.

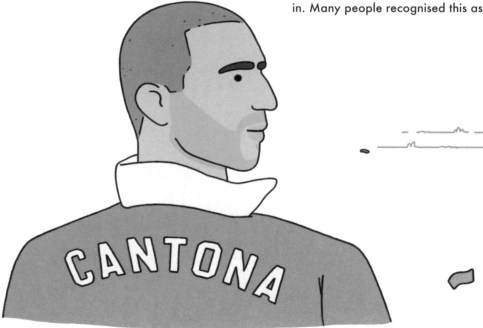

THE CANTONA LOOK-AROUND

Eric Cantona was great at football. On 21st December 1996, at a chilly Old Trafford, King Eric scored the most glorious of chips, leaving the goalkeeper to watch the ball dive-bomb into the very top corner of the goal, nestling into the net. Eric knew he was a special player and he was too cool to celebrate an unbelievable goal. Goals are just what he does. Instead, he stood perfectly still and then looked around as if to say, 'Yes, you did just see that. Believe your eyes'.

BALOTELLI'S 'WHY ALWAYS ME?'

There are lots of stories about the crazy things that Italian player Mario Balotelli has done during his career as a footballer. Some of are them true, some of them false. Whatever happened during his time at Manchester City, all of the attention always seemed to end up on Super Mario. When he scored the first goal in a 6-1 win for City over Manchester United in 2011, he lifted up his shirt to reveal a message on his underlayer that read, 'WHY ALWAYS ME?' Because you're unique, Mario, and we love you for it.

THE CROUCH ROBOT

England player Peter Crouch is 6ft 7in tall, which is over 2 metres. Due to his height, spectators often said he looked awkward and uncoordinated. When Crouchy scored for England against Hungary in a pre-World Cup friendly in 2006, he decided to show the world that he was actually very coordinated indeed, thank you very much, and performed a robot dance in front of the whole world.

THE KLINSMANN

In 1990, Jürgen Klinsmann scored three goals for Germany at the World Cup. He had a very good tournament, but it is not his goals at the tournament that are remembered, it is his diving. In 1990s England, diving was considered a terrible form of cheating. So when Klinsmann arrived in England to play his first game for Tottenham Hotspur against Sheffield Wednesday in 1994, the crowd booed him. Klinsmann was a very talented striker and he scored a powerful header, after which he ran over to the side of the pitch and did a big dive onto the turf. Even the Wednesday fans laughed.

THE GOGGLES

Ellen White, the England international striker whose goals at the World Cup in 2019 saw England progress through the stages, has a trademark celebration: The Goggles. Ellen is from Aylesbury in England, and has played for Arsenal, Leeds, Birmingham, Notts County, Chelsea and Manchester City, but she loves watching German football. After seeing Anthony Modeste put his hands around his eyes to make hand-goggles, Ellen started doing it herself. In fact, she scores so many goals that she does The Goggles a lot.

THE BIGGEST, THE BEST AND THE WEIRDEST

BIGGEST STADIUMS

DID YOU KNOW that the five biggest football stadiums (in terms of capacity) are in five different continents?

The **RUNGRADO 1ST OF MAY STADIUM** in Pyongyang, North Korea, holds 114,000 people. - ASIA

The **MELBOURNE CRICKET GROUND** in Australia, home to the Socceroos, holds 100,024 people. - OCEANIA

The **CAMP NOU** in Barcelona, Spain, holds 99,354 people. - EUROPE

The **FNB STADIUM** in Johannesburg, South Africa, holds 94,736 people. - AFRICA

The **ROSE BOWL STADIUM** in Pasadena, California, USA, holds 90,888 people. - NORTH AMERICA

BIGGEST SCORE

On Halloween 2002, two Madagascan teams were playing each other in a play-off tournament. SO l'Emyrne were annoyed, as they thought that the referees had treated them unfairly in the previous games. They intentionally lost the game, going down 149-0 to their biggest rivals AS Adema.

149-0

BIGGEST CROWDS

199,854 spectators attended the 1950 World Cup final between Brazil and Uruguay at the Maracanã Stadium in Rio De Janeiro. At least 20,000 of the spectators didn't even have tickets.

DARREN BENT DOES LOVE TO BE BESIDE THE SEASIDE

In 2009, Sunderland were playing Liverpool in a Premier League match at the Stadium of Light. Five minutes into the game, Sunderland striker Darren Bent hit a low, pretty tame shot at goal. Liverpool's goalie, Pepe Reina got down to gather the ball into his arms, but then something strange happened.

A Liverpool fan had brought a big red beach ball with him to the game. He threw the beach ball up in the air, and the wind blew it onto the pitch just at the moment that Bent took his shot. The football bounced off the beach ball and past Pepe Reina, who must've been wondering what on earth had just happened. The referee allowed the goal to stand and was later relegated to the Championship (the league below the Premier League) because of this. Sunderland went on to win the game 1-0, and the unfortunate Liverpool fan still feels guilty.

LARGEST PLAYER

The tallest footballer in the world is Dulwich Hamlet's goalkeeper, Simon Bloch Jørgensen, who is 6ft 10in tall. Goalkeepers tend to be taller than outfield players, but if you're a goalkeeper and are shorter than your friends, do not fear. Many people consider Reading's greatest ever goalkeeper to be Steve Death, who was 5ft 7in tall. There are two or three goalkeepers who were slightly shorter than Steve Death, but he also has probably the most rock 'n' roll name a footballer has ever had. One more time: Steve Death.

SMALLEST PLAYER

The shortest male footballers on record are Élton José Xavier Gomes and Daniel Alberto Villalva Barrios from Brazil and Argentina respectively. They are both just over 5 feet. It goes to show that height doesn't matter, as long as you practise your skills and put in lots of effort.

MOST HAT-TRICKS

It is said that Pelé scored 92 career hat-tricks. Some of these may have been in non-competitive matches but we'll give him the benefit of the doubt.

MOST SENT OFF PLAYER

The player who has received the most red cards in their career is Colombian defender/midfielder Gerardo Alberto Bedoya Múnera, who was sent off 46 times. To put that into context, the player with the second most red cards is Cyril Rool with 27.

ODDEST RED CARDS

Lots of football players are superstitious. Many players have lucky boots or shin pads. When Mukura Victory were playing Rayon Sport in the Rwandan Premier League in 2016, Victory's striker Moussa Camara was feeling particularly unlucky. He had missed several easy opportunities to score, and so he took matters into his own hands by placing a strange object on the goalposts and, apparently, casting a spell. The referee booked him for witchcraft, but Camara went on to score... mysterious!

Swedish player Adam Lindin Ljungkvist was once shown a second yellow card for farting during a reserve team game in Sweden. Ljungkvist states he had an upset stomach, but the referee disagreed. The ref said that Ljungkvist had purposefully provoked an opponent by farting towards them, and sent the defender off.

STIR-FRIED AEROPLANE

As we have already mentioned, fans use some clever, funny and downright ridiculous words and phrases to describe things that happen in football (see p.9). There is special football lingo in every language and here are some of our favourite phrases, or idioms, from around the world.

炒飛機 – STIR-FRIED AEROPLANE (CHINA)

A phrase used to describe a shot that has gone far wide or over. In English, we might say that the shot has been 'spooned'.

IMURI – VACUUM CLEANER (FINLAND)

In Finland, if you're a rubbish goalkeeper, then you'll be described as a vacuum cleaner: because you can't stop things from being sucked into the goal.

泥臭い – SMELLING OF MUD (JAPAN)

Not all goals are beautiful. In fact, loads aren't beautiful. They're scored by really forcing the ball over the line, something we might call a goalmouth scramble. In Japan, if it's a goal through determination rather than beauty, then it's described as smelling of mud.

HACER LA CAMA – TO MAKE THE BED (ARGENTINA)

Sometimes, a group of players will decide that their manager isn't doing the right thing, and essentially gang up on him. Really hammer him, stop trying, spread rumours. In Argentina, it's described as making his bed: 'Go to sleep, manager'.

NA BANHEIRA – IN THE BATHTUB (BRAZIL)

If you are caught offside, this can be very annoying for your teammates, especially if they've worked hard to get to a position where they can play a pass to you. In Brazil, if this happened they would say you are taking a bath because it is as though you are lazing around and not helping.

POTET – POTATO (NORWAY)

Potatoes are great. You can mash them, boil them, roast them and turn them into chips. So, in Norway, if you're good at everything on the pitch and able to play in all positions, then you're a potato. A humble, versatile potato.

JEP NEST (TRINIDAD AND TOBAGO)

A jack spania, or a jep, is the Caribbean name for a wasp. Wasps like to nest in the top corners of things. So, if you shoot into the top corner of the net in Trinidad and Tobago, the ball has gone into the jep nest.

NABRAT NA SANE – TO TAKE SOMEONE ON A SLEIGH RIDE (CZECH REPUBLIC)

Sometimes slide tackles can go wrong, and you get completely wiped out by one with your legs in the air, your back bent and your head somewhere else. In the Czech Republic, they say this is as though Santa has picked you up on his sleigh and off you go, all around the houses.

MINESTRA RISCALDATA – REHEATED SOUP (ITALY)

There are certain football managers who go back to a club after they've already worked there before. In Italy, they'd describe this as reheated soup.

BAPTISER – TO BAPTISE (CAMEROON)

It's really annoying if a player scoops the ball over your head. It makes you feel silly. If it happens to you in Cameroon, they'll say you've been baptised.

MORE THAN THE GAME

You may think that football is just about what happens on the pitch: the magnificent goals, the soaring saves and the big tackles that echo all around the stadium. But it's not. Much of what makes football, football, is the whole culture surrounding the game and the dedicated people who make the games possible. At a football match, the referee is as important as the striker. At a club, the nutritionist might make as much difference as the defensive coach. And the spirit of the crowd contributes as much to the atmosphere as the players.

RESPECTING THE REF

The referee, just like you, loves football. It is easy to forget that when you are playing or watching a game, but it is true. The decisions that they make allow us to play the game properly and fairly. It is essential to understand why and how they make the decisions they make and how they signal what their decision is.

IF SOMEONE IS OFFSIDE...

The assistant referee, who runs in line with the last defender, will raise their flag parallel with the ground. The referee will give a little toot on their whistle and wave their arm along the offside line. Keep playing until you hear that whistle, though: sometimes the ref will overrule the assistant refs.

IF THERE'S A GOAL...

The referee will blow their whistle and point to the centre-spot to show that the game now needs to be restarted by a kick-off.

IF THERE'S A DIRECT FREE KICK...

The referee will blow their whistle. Then they will point in the direction in which the team who have been awarded the free kick are kicking.

IF THERE'S AN INDIRECT FREE KICK...

The referee will blow their whistle and point straight towards the sky. An indirect free kick is a free kick from which you must pass the ball – you cannot shoot. They're awarded for offences such as a handball, a back pass that the goalkeeper picks up, or offensive language or dissent shown towards the referee.

IF THERE'S A THROW-IN...

The ref will blow their whistle and point in the kicking direction of the team who has won the throw-in.

IF THERE'S A GOAL KICK...

The ref will blow the whistle and point at the six-yard box.

IF THERE'S A CORNER...

The referee will point towards the corner and the assistant referee will point their flag towards the corner. If you score direct from a corner, it's called an olimpico.

IF THERE'S A HANDBALL...

If you purposely play the ball with your hand or arm, the other team will be awarded an indirect free kick or even a penalty if you're in your own penalty area.

Goalkeepers can obviously use their hands and arms, but only inside their own penalty area. If they handle the ball outside of the penalty area, an indirect free kick will be awarded to the opposition and the goalkeeper may be sent off!

IF THERE'S INJURY TIME...

The amount of injury time is calculated by the assistant referee, who writes it up on a board. If a game is stopped for ten minutes because of injuries during the match, ten minutes will be added on to the end of the 90-minute-game.

A RED CARD...

If you foul another player or commit a serious offence then you will be given one of these and it means you need to leave the pitch immediately.

PIERLUIGI COLLINA

Pierluigi Collina was a really famous Italian referee. He was famous because of his shiny bald head and electric-blue eyes that made him absolutely terrifying. No player dared to argue with him and he was the first referee to feature on the front cover of a Pro Evolution Soccer game.

A YELLOW CARD...

This is a warning. If you do something bad, you'll get one of these. And if you get two, you will be sent off.

THE OTHER JOBS

You don't have to be a footballer to be a crucial member of the football club. Lots of people contribute to a match and in the run-up to a match. Here are a few of the important jobs that go on behind the scenes.

THE GROUNDSMAN

Football pitches look beautiful, don't they? They need around-the-clock care to keep them level and make sure that the grass is hydrated, green and luscious. If you like gardening and football, this could be the job for you.

THE KITMAN

Sparkling clean kits and boots don't appear magically. It is someone's job to wash, iron and fold them. The kitman is a very important person – without them, players wouldn't look as smart as they do.

THE NUTRITIONIST

This person tells the players what to eat for breakfast, lunch, dinner and everything in between so that their bodies work like well-oiled machines when it comes to the big game.

THE PHYSIOTHERAPIST

Most often shortened to 'the physio', these professionals are there to treat injured players. You might see them rush onto the pitch to tend to a player who's just been involved in a nasty tackle or an awkward fall. You might see them struggling with a stretcher to take a player into the dressing rooms for treatment. They are highly skilled and very important.

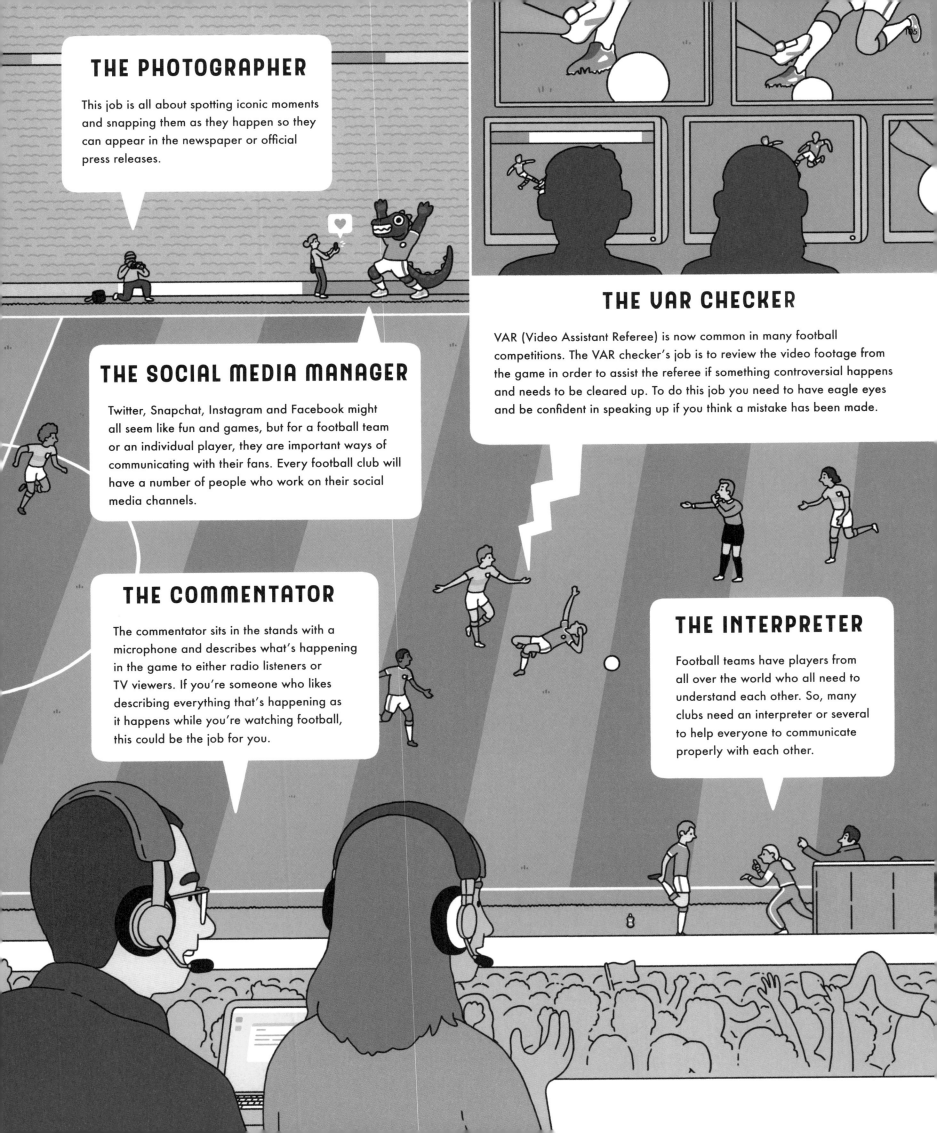

THE PHOTOGRAPHER

This job is all about spotting iconic moments and snapping them as they happen so they can appear in the newspaper or official press releases.

THE VAR CHECKER

VAR (Video Assistant Referee) is now common in many football competitions. The VAR checker's job is to review the video footage from the game in order to assist the referee if something controversial happens and needs to be cleared up. To do this job you need to have eagle eyes and be confident in speaking up if you think a mistake has been made.

THE SOCIAL MEDIA MANAGER

Twitter, Snapchat, Instagram and Facebook might all seem like fun and games, but for a football team or an individual player, they are important ways of communicating with their fans. Every football club will have a number of people who work on their social media channels.

THE COMMENTATOR

The commentator sits in the stands with a microphone and describes what's happening in the game to either radio listeners or TV viewers. If you're someone who likes describing everything that's happening as it happens while you're watching football, this could be the job for you.

THE INTERPRETER

Football teams have players from all over the world who all need to understand each other. So, many clubs need an interpreter or several to help everyone to communicate properly with each other.

THE MATCH DAY

If you are going to watch a football match, whoever you're with, whoever you're watching play and wherever you're watching it, it is an amazing experience. Around the world, everyone experiences football matches in different ways. Many customs are similar, others are very specific to a particular place. There will always be a pitch and a ball and two teams, but sometimes there won't be a stand and sometimes there will be four stands that hold 100,000 people. Some people will have a pre-match hot dog, and others might have a burrito. All of these elements come together to make match day wonderful. There is a guide to what you might see, smell and hear.

LEAVING HOME

Getting ready for the match is important: you need to dress appropriately...

You may want to wear your lucky scarf, or shirt or pants. Although unfortunately, your team can still lose even if you are wearing all three lucky items.

Remember your tickets!

THE JOURNEY TO THE GAME

If you are driving to the game with your family or your friends, you can tune into the pre-match build-up on the radio.

If you're catching the train, you might bump into lots of other football fans and chat about what you think is going to happen during the match and what you thought of the last game.

If you're taking the bus or coach to the game, especially an away game, groups of fans will sing and cheer all the way to the match. This is lots of fun if you're a fan but probably a nightmare if you're a coach driver.

If you're walking to the match, listen as the noise of the crowd grows louder and louder as you approach!

PRE-MATCH FOOD

There are all sorts of pre, during and post-match foods around the globe. Here are some of the best:

Mexico Noodles with chilli and lime. People will come to your seat and sell you noodles in many football grounds in Mexico.

Russia & Spain Sunflower seeds and peanuts. These healthy little snacks are very popular and as you leave the stadium, your feet crunch over the shells like fresh snow.

United Kingdom Pies. Hot pies are a classic football food in the UK, probably because they are very warming on a cold day spent outside!

Germany *Currywurst*. This is a boiled and fried sausage covered in curry sauce. They are utterly *wunderschön*.

Belgium *Frites* & mayonnaise. Belgium is famous for its *frites*, also known as chips or fries.

USA Hot dogs. These are a match day staple in the US, served with fried onions, mustard and ketchup. Perfect.

PROGRAMME AND SCARF SELLERS

On your way into the ground, you may see people selling programmes or scarves. Programmes often have lots of pictures and interviews with players, or a message from the team manager. They also have a list on the back of them with the names of all the players and their squad number, which makes it easier to figure out who scored that amazing goal if you're sitting miles away from the pitch. Scarves and programmes are great souvenirs to have from a football match but they are not as important as your memories.

STEWARD

These guys make sure everything runs smoothly at the game and that everyone behaves. Important.

STADIUM ANNOUNCER

This person has a microphone connected to big speakers in the stadium. They'll announce the teams and goals and provide a bit of entertainment at half time.

TURNSTILE OPERATOR

You'll have to give this person your ticket. Although, more and more often stadiums have replaced the operators with machine turnstiles.

MASCOT

A person dressed in a big, often fluffy costume that represents your team. They are usually good at gymnastics, or running, or throwing prizes into the stands.

THE CROWD

Football crowds are described in many ways by many people. Some people think they are like one huge family and others say they are like churchgoers at their chapel and others say they are a bunch of hooligans. One thing we can agree on is that without them, football would be nothing.

Songs and chants, generally, come and go with changing players and managers. Many of them are witty or funny, but the best ones are simple and timeless. If you can think of a chant or song that applies to the team regardless of who the players or managers are, then you're onto a winner. There are some, however, that remain constant.

'Walk on, walk on
With hope in your heart
And you'll never walk alone
You'll never walk alone.'

LIVERPOOL *YOU'LL NEVER WALK ALONE*

This is a song of togetherness winning over adversity. Liverpool fans sing it to a crescendo before every game they play. It has inspired many a famous win for the reds.

As well as the chants, the crowd express themselves with banners, posters, tifos and wild dancing performances. Look out for these on terraces around the world.

ICELAND NATIONAL TEAM *THE VIKING CLAP*

Some chants have no words at all. At World Cup 2018 in Russia, the Icelandic fans often performed the thunderclap to spur on their team. The fans would clap once, all at the same time. One mega-loud clap. Then they'd do it again, leaving a shorter and shorter gap between each clap, speeding up, until the whole crowd was clapping, apparently like Vikings.

THE POZNAN / GRECQUE

A form of celebration where row upon row of fans turn their backs to the game, link arms and jump up and down at the same time. It looks like a huge wave, and it originated in Poland in 1961. Manchester City played a team called Poznan in 2010, saw their fans doing it and decided to steal it.

THE YELLOW WALL

328ft long and 131ft high, Borussia Dortmund's stadium Westfalenstadion has a single stand full of 24,450 fans called Die Gelbe Wand – The Yellow Wall. The noise it makes is phenomenal, the colours are next level, and the huge banners that the fans make for each game, called tifos, are the best in the world.

DOING THE DAI

Llanelli Town are a semi-professional Welsh team, and Dai Chappell is their superfan. Born in 1944, Dai has gone to every Llanelli game for 25 years and is famous for his celebration. He often stands behind the goal on his own and throws both of his arms to the sky each time Llanelli score.

FOOTBALL SONGS IN POP CULTURE

Football songs have occasionally become popular beyond football and made it into the charts. This is especially common in World Cup years when nations adopt a song as their anthem for the tournament. *Three Lions* by Baddiel, Skinner and The Lightning Seeds, *World In Motion* by New Order (featuring John Barnes' infamous rapping skills) and *Nessun Dorma*, originally from the Puccini opera *Turandot*, are among the most popular of these.

INDEX

The names, trademarks and logos of the named entities and brands profiled in this book are the property of their respective owners and are used solely for identification purposes. This book is a publication of Quarto Publishing plc and it has not been prepared, approved, endorsed or licensed by any other brand, person or entity.

Inspiring | Educating | Creating | Entertaining

Brimming with creative inspiration, how-to projects, and useful information to enrich your everyday life, Quarto Knows is a favorite destination for those pursuing their interests and passions. Visit our site and dig deeper with our books into your area of interest: Quarto Creates, Quarto Cooks, Quarto Homes, Quarto Lives, Quarto Drives, Quarto Explores, Quarto Gifts, or Quarto Kids.

The Big Book of Football by Mundial © 2020 Quarto Publishing plc
Text © 2020 Mundial
Illustrations © 2020 Damien Weighill

First published in 2020 by Wide Eyed Editions, an imprint of The Quarto Group
The Old Brewery, 6 Blundell Street, London N7 9BH, United Kingdom.
T (0)20 7700 6700 F (0)20 7700 8066 **www.QuartoKnows.com**

A catalogue record for this book is available from the British Library.

ISBN 978-0-7112-5820-4
The illustrations were created digitally
Set in Mexcellent 3D, Futura and Hipton Sans

Published by Georgia Amson-Bradshaw
Designed by Myrto Dimitrakoulia
Edited by Lucy Brownridge

Manufactured in Guangdong, China CC112019

9 8 7 6 5 4 3 2 1

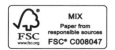

MIX
Paper from
responsible sources
FSC® C008047